HOPE, HEART, AND THE HUMANITIES

HOPE, HEART, AND THE HUMANITIES

How a Free College Course
Is Changing Lives

EDITED BY JEAN CHENEY AND L. JACKSON NEWELL

Hikmet Sidney Loe, Jeff Metcalf, and Bridget M. Newell

UNIVERSITY OF UTAH PRESS
Salt Lake City, Utah

The Defiance House Man colophon is a registered trademark of
the University of Utah Press. It is based on a four-foot-tall Ancient
Puebloan pictograph (late PIII) near Glen Canyon, Utah.

20 19 18 17 16   1 2 3 4 5

LIBRARY OF CONGRESS CATALOGING-IN-PUBLICATION DATA
Names: Cheney, Jean, 1947- editor. | Newell, L. Jackson, 1938- editor.
Title: Hope, heart, and the humanities : how a free college course is
    changing lives / edited by Jean Cheney and L. Jackson Newell ; Hikmet
    Sidney Loe, Jeff Metcalf, and Bridget M. Newell [authors].
Description: Salt Lake City : University of Utah Press, [2016] | Includes
    bibliographical references.
Identifiers: LCCN 2016025382| ISBN 9781607815280 (pbk. : alk. paper) |
    ISBN 9781607815273 (ebook)
Subjects: LCSH: Humanities—Study and teaching—United States. | Education,
    Humanistic—United States. | Poor—Education—United States. | Adult
    education—Study and teaching—United States.
Classification: LCC AZ183.U5 H67 2016 | DDC 001.3071/073—dc23 LC record
available at https://lccn.loc.gov/2016025382

Printed and bound by Edwards Brothers Malloy, Inc., Ann Arbor, Michigan

For those who
champion the humanities
as though our future depends on it.

CONTENTS

FIGURES

FOREWORD

When I was growing up, I was captivated by a book called *The Family of Man,* a collection of black-and-white photographs of people from all over the world caught in the act of praying and playing, marrying and mourning. On the page that I returned to again and again were unsettling portraits from the Great Depression and, at the bottom, a quote from Virgil: "What region of the earth is not full of our calamities?" I guess you could say this was one of my early encounters with the humanities, which is to say I had come upon a piece of art that got under my skin and changed me.

There is a purpose, of course, for learning coding and calculus and how to balance a checkbook. But hooray for the subjects that move us to tears, or move us to action, or simply make us sit still and reflect on our lives and the lives of others.

So I was intrigued in 2005 when Jean Cheney first told me about the Venture Course in the Humanities and its unlikely students—many of them trying to navigate lives full of compounding calamities—who would now have a chance to study history, philosophy, and literature. For free.

I was a newspaper reporter at the time, so from September until their graduation the next spring, I followed those students, some of them recently homeless or in prison. I watched sixteen adults read Neruda, become excited over Vermeer, contemplate existentialism, and discuss what it means to have "a good life."

"I used to believe that, because I was poor, the world was not open to me," one of the students remarked near the end of the course. "I thought you had to have the right ticket and the right shoes." Before she started the Venture program, she had been unsure of herself and her future, but after eight months of classes, she had a different view: "You can walk into a museum," she said, "and you don't have to hide from anyone." The next fall, she enrolled in college.

Venture is now a decade old and has enrolled more than four hundred students. *Hope, Heart, and the Humanities* chronicles, with honesty and grace, their way forward.

PREFACE

Should you read this book? Yes, if you care about education, especially education in the humanities—history, philosophy, art, literature—those subjects that help us understand the full reach of human experience and expand the ways we see the world. "Only by studying this world can we hope to shape how it shapes us," writes Mark Slouka in "Dehumanized" in *Harper's;* "only by attempting to understand what used to be called, in a less embarrassed age, 'the human condition,' can we hope to make our condition more human, not less." *Yes.*

Much has been written about the importance of STEM subjects in public and higher education. Science, math, engineering, and technology are powerful tools for investigating and influencing the outer, objective world. But by themselves, they do not help us understand the complex human world we live in. They may be good for our GDP, but they do little to strengthen our democracy, nor can they help us understand ourselves or one another. For these, we need the humanities. They're essential to us as individuals and as a community. Without a people who know American history and the founding principles of our country, who can think critically and work through complex questions, America's still-fragile experiment of self-government may be in trouble.

This is also a book for anyone worried about inequities in America and looking for ways to create opportunities for those struggling in poverty. It is for readers interested in innovative approaches to college teaching, especially new ways to teach older, nontraditional students, including immigrants and refugees.

You are about to read the story of a humanities course in Utah that is changing the lives of its students and faculty. It is one of a national network of free courses—all adapted from the same template—that serve people living on low incomes. In Utah, it is called the "Venture Course"; in Illinois, the "Odyssey Project"; in Oregon, "Humanities in Perspective"; and in many other places, the "Clemente Course" after the program begun by the late Earl Shorris in 1995 in the Roberto Clemente Community Center in New York City. Whatever their name, courses similar to Venture exist in ten states as well as Canada and Australia. (For more information about the Clemente course network, visit www.clementecourse.com. For a history of the program, see Earl Shorris, *Riches for the Poor: The Clemente Course in the Humanities.)*

In the fall of 2015, President Barack Obama honored this network with the 2014 National Humanities Medal at a ceremony in the White House. The president praised Clemente courses for bringing "free humanities education to thousands of men and women, enriching their lives and broadening their horizons." While each Clemente course is slightly different, all share similar goals, structure, and spirit. All try to help students develop their inner lives and autonomy and to encourage engagement in their communities. Although Clemente courses do not succeed with all students who enroll, the impact can be life changing for those who stay. This is the story of one of them and the difference it is making.

As white, middle-class, middle-aged Americans, we were keenly aware from the outset that we had much to learn from the students we would meet in the Venture Course. Predominantly people of color and from diverse religious and cultural backgrounds, and all living on low incomes, they taught us gently and generously. A decade later—as awareness of the impact of privilege, race, culture, and class has sharpened in us—we are grateful for the rich experiences that Venture students have brought to the classroom and the charity and patience they have shown. The way their learning and ours grew is part of the story this book tells.

For one year, three of us—Jeff, Jean, and Jack—kept teaching journals, noting student conversations and interactions. Sometimes we wrote these notes during class while students were writing or reading, sometimes immediately afterward, when class discussions were fresh in our minds. These notes helped us recapture what happened much more closely than would have been possible long after the class concluded. Even so, some of the described conversations are approximations. They reflect student thoughts and echo their voices but are not always exact quotations.

To protect students' identities and privacy, we have changed their names, unless they had shared their work and their stories previously through print and electronic publications, the Utah Humanities (formerly the Utah Humanities Council) website, or a public exhibit. We have described scenes and conversations to the best of our memories and notes. No student described is a composite, and no scenes were invented.

A word about authorship: this book was in gestation for more than seven years. Fairly early on our journey with Venture, we knew we wanted to tell the story, to share the moving experiences we were having in the classroom, but the writing did not come easily. We had different writing styles, reflecting our individual ways of teaching. We wanted to include student voices but also protect their privacy. Uncertainty about the way to shape the story and problems coordinating our efforts brought us to the brink of abandoning the whole project. In the end, however, writing these pages deepened our understanding of what we do, whom we teach, and why we invest so much effort in making Venture work.

To add vitality to the narratives of our separate teaching experiences, we wrote in the first person, but we also needed to set our Venture Course within its contemporary and historical contexts, explain its origins, and describe our ways of working together.

To accomplish these goals, each of us wrote a chapter solely about teaching his or her segment of the two-semester course: Jeff Metcalf on literature, Hikmet Loe on art history, Jean Cheney on critical writing, Bridget Newell on philosophy, and Jack Newell on American history (the Newells are not related). Then Jean took the lead in drafting the preface and writing chapters 1, 2, 9, and 10, with Jeff and Jack contributing. Jeff and Jean wrote the introduction, and Jeff wrote chapter 8 with passages contributed by the other four authors. Bridget added the critiques of Clemente that appear in chapter 2. Jeff contributed a description of the Humanities in Focus sequel to our Venture Course described in chapter 10, and Jack crafted the epilogue.

Pulling the disparate parts together, Jean and Jack edited the entire volume, coordinating the chapters, writing what needed to be added to integrate and complete the story, and grooming the whole.

In the end, the words from Venture students themselves that appear throughout the book may have the most resonance. We are indebted to them for the insights and wisdom they shared with us.

INTRODUCTION

I do not know where I found the courage to take this course. I was divorced, had been homeless with my three children, and had "nothing." We had survived going in and out of shelters and living out of an old car, heating food on its radiator. I did not realize that by dwelling for a time at the bottom, I had taken myself out of humanity. Living too long away tends to make a heart grow cold. Somewhere I dared to want to be warm again. I dared to want to fill the nothingness.

—BARBRA, *VENTURE GRADUATE*

We walk across a large plaza toward a long, graceful ramp leading to the rooftop garden of the Salt Lake City Public Library. With its plaza and amphitheater outdoors and bookstores and coffee shops inside, this new library isn't like the ones the students in our group have known. Before tonight, most have never set foot on its grounds. As we walk up the ramp, we can see through the library's five-story wall of glass to people seated at computers or meeting in small groups, sitting together, their heads bent toward each other in conversation. This is a living, breathing, public library.

It is orientation night for the Venture Course in the Humanities. Thirty of us—twenty-five students and five faculty members—are making an annual pilgrimage. We don't hold classes at the library, but it is where we begin the journey because it symbolizes the values we believe Venture embodies. Like this library at the heart of the city, Venture is a crossroads, a place where people access books, great ideas, history, and conversation—where,

1

if they are willing, they can challenge themselves safely. Like using the library, there is no cost to participate in Venture, but what you find there can change your life. We walk with our new students in this public meeting space—a group of strangers, each a little nervous.

As she walks up the ramp, Ella[1] looks across the Salt Lake Valley to the dark flanks of the Wasatch Mountains, which seem closer than usual tonight. "Did you live near mountains in your country?" asks Jean Cheney, who teaches critical writing to Venture students. Ella wears a long, flowered indigo dress and matching head scarf. She is a tiny woman from Sierra Leone with small features and bright eyes. "Oh, yes," she says. "But at night, you could see these little fires on the mountains. All these fires, every night!"

On the roof, we enter a large garden of tall grasses and perennials. Most of them native to Utah, the grasses blow gently in a late summer breeze. We walk around and enjoy a 360-degree view of the great valley, the city stretching out for miles to the south, rimmed in three directions by mountains. In the west, the sun is sinking into the desert, sending rose-colored arrows of light through the clouds.

Soon we turn away from the vistas and toward each other. We assemble in a rough circle, some on the metal chairs scattered about, others sitting on the ground. Already we begin to feel less like anxious strangers, more like the beginning of a group. Our backs are to the unknown, and our faces are attentive to each other in anticipation—of something.

Much will happen in the next half hour as, one by one, each of us answers the question, "Why are you here?" For many gathered in the circle, the idea of attending a college course in the humanities twice a week for a full academic year is daunting. Overwhelming. There is no sense of easy expectation or entitlement here.

These students are not like the ones we see during the day in our college classrooms. About a third of this year's class are refugees from war-torn countries who, we know from their application essays, have experienced horrific events in their lives and somehow survived. Many have lost family members to war. Salt Lake City is an official International Refugee City and welcomes hundreds of refugees each year. Others, American born, have equally painful stories. Addictions, violence, extreme poverty, prison, homelessness, discrimination have all left their scars. We know that those gathered here share a common hope. Theirs is the simple dream of wanting to start again.

The Venture Course is the first step toward something they can't quite name but fervently want. They are humble and beautiful people, but, for many reasons, they have not been included. Being at the library on the first evening of class is an act of bravery and faith. As their teachers, we are keenly aware that they're taking a tremendous gamble, and from this first night, we do all we can to honor our end of this compact: to start wherever they are, help them on this journey, and teach them our passions.

Jeff Metcalf, the literature teacher, welcomes us. In his early sixties, Jeff is a writer of plays and nonfiction and professor of English and education at the University of Utah. His easy manner and warm, joking humor connect with the students immediately. Jeff invites a tall, dark-haired man to tell us his name and why he decided to take the Venture Course. The man is sitting on the ground, staring intently at the matted grass beneath him.

A few of the faculty met him earlier on the library's plaza. His nametag proclaimed that he was Kasim. In clear English, he told us that he was from Iraq and had been in the U.S. for three years. "Have you been back to Iraq?" Jean asked. "No," he answered. In the awkward silence that followed, she recognized that it was a thoughtless question.

Now Kasim does not look up, and his complexion is coloring. "He is too shy to speak," the man next to him says. "He is embarrassed," Ahmed explains for his friend, then introduces himself, filling the silence.

Ahmed is also from Iraq. A middle-aged man with lively, dark eyes, he speaks precise, careful English. He tells us he wants to continue the education that his forced departure from Iraq interrupted. But he doesn't know the system here, he says, and he doesn't have any money.

What students share in this circle often expands on the stories they already shared with us in their application essays or interviews. Sometimes, in this garden, they speak harder truths. Several years ago, Cecilia, a tall middle-aged woman from Tonga with thick brown hair coiled on her head, stood in the garden, straightened her spine, held her head high, and told us about coming to the U.S. with five children to educate. She had abandoned her dream of attending college when she married at eighteen. This was the first time in her life—the only time, she said, choking back tears— that she had ever decided to do something for herself. "I am so grateful to be here," she confessed.

Holding orientation in a rooftop garden of a city library is an odd way to begin a college humanities course. But then this isn't a typical course.

The Venture Course in the Humanities is advertised in a blue brochure as a "journey that can change your life." The brochure's cover shows a silhouetted figure standing on a mountaintop, looking up at the sky. Applicants to Venture tell us that they're seeking something, although many are unsure what. They know from this blue brochure that they will study five humanities disciplines and join a "community of learners" for two semesters. If they complete the course requirements, they will earn eight credits from Westminster College, a small, widely respected, liberal-arts college in Salt Lake City.

But the credits are not part of any academic program. They're an endorsement, an incentive for some. We have learned that, for most students, the credits are not the goal. Starting over is. To be welcomed at the human table for exploration, conversation, and sharing ideas is why they come. Or it's simply for the joy in learning, to pick up an education that was cut off too early.

Venture recruits students from the entire Salt Lake Valley. The only requirements are to be at least eighteen, living on a low income, and able to read a newspaper in English. An applicant must also be willing to commit to eight months of meeting on Tuesday and Thursday evenings for two hours. Aspiring students submit an application and write a short essay explaining why they want to join the course. They interview with one of the faculty members, which gives us the opportunity to assess their commitment, general mental health, and language skills. After these simple steps, they are in.

Once admitted, students stay together for eight months. They experience five teachers and five subjects over those months: literature and art history in the fall, philosophy and American history in the spring, and critical writing classes during both semesters.

In their application essays or during the required interview, students tell us some version of "I know that this may be the last chance I have to turn around my life," or "I want to set a good example for my children," or "I used to like to read and write, but it's been a long time, and I don't know how to find my way back." They tell us that, yes, they want to study the humanities—these subjects attract them—but we soon realize that the figure on the mountaintop in the blue brochure attracts them, too. Many live with fading dreams and fear there is little time left to rescue them. Others work in dead-end jobs and want something better for their futures. Most know that they have good minds and want to use them and to be useful. They're willing to gamble on this thing called Venture. Tuition is free, and books, child care, and transportation are all provided. After their interviews, they shake our hands and say, "Yes, I want to do this."

The five professors come from three institutions: the University of Utah, Westminster College, and Utah Humanities. We are a small band that meets frequently, in coffee shops or each other's backyards, to discuss our experiences as teachers and ways to improve the Venture experience. Rather than an extension of our day jobs, we see our Venture teaching as something exceptional. We come to it—often tired at the end of a packed workday—and leave rejuvenated, marveling at the way, once again, something nearly magical has happened in the classroom. We know that Venture offers us a chance to connect with people we would probably never meet otherwise in ways that are surprising and meaningful to all of us. It allows us to spread our passions by igniting them in these students who have bravely stepped forth to take this chance. To each of us, Venture feels like important, meaningful work.

At the orientation in the library's garden, Jack Newell, who will be teaching American history during the second semester, explains more about Venture. In his early seventies, with short, curly, salt-and-pepper hair, Jack sits cross-legged on the ground. President emeritus of Deep Springs College, a selective, highly innovative liberal-arts college in eastern California, Jack is also professor emeritus at the University of Utah, where he teaches in the Honors College. "We meet to begin our venture together in a significant location," he says. "In fact, it is a doubly symbolic place. We are perched atop one of the finest public libraries in the West." Jack speaks in a deep, sure voice. Every face locks on him.

> Below us is a huge storehouse of knowledge—contained in millions of books lodged on shelves and in hundreds of computers—from which we will draw richly throughout the coming year. Beyond our gaze is the larger world. Lift your eyes above the surrounding peaks to consider the whole of humanity. Others beckon us to expand our understandings beyond this particular place, or the one we may have recently come from, to become more fully alive, more vital participants in our communities. What a place this is to begin!

The students are stirred by Jack's words. He has made them aware that beneath us—tucked and buried inside the broad, muscular shoulders of this library—are human questions, answered and unanswered. This idea, so powerfully voiced, gives the students permission to reveal their excitement. Their faces begin to soften as they continue to introduce themselves.

We learn that Kasim wants to be an engineer. Stella wants to get an education so that her son will have a better life than she has had. Ella wants to be a nurse. Carlos wants to be a teacher. Juanita, a tall woman from Haiti, dressed in a caftan and head scarf, explains she has always wanted to be a writer, a poet. She is a poet now but wants to be better. Into the invisible fire at the center of our circle, one by one, our students lay their dreams.

On this warm, late summer evening, we have twenty-five eager souls. By the end of the first semester in late December, six or eight students will have dropped the course. Some will e-mail or phone us to say their hours have changed at work, or they have to take care of a sick brother or deal with a child who has become addicted to drugs. Others will not last the year, and we will never know why. They will just stop coming to class. Given the circumstances of their lives, of trying to balance family responsibilities with one or two jobs and still attend classes at the end of a long workday, reality dictates their choices. Old demons of addictions or the vestiges of years of abuse sometimes surface, too, making this rigorous course too much to continue. The frustration of reading difficult texts in a foreign language discourages some. As a faculty, we understand these reasons but are stirred by every loss.

Those who stay will finish the course as different people than they are in this circle tonight: more confident that they are powerful; less certain about some beliefs, more certain of others. They will know they can make things happen in their lives and the lives of others. We will watch as they change, reclaiming parts of themselves that they had lost. If this group is like others, they will become a family of learners by December, caring for and about one another. By April, a young man from Iraq who cannot bring himself to speak tonight may become the keynote speaker at his graduation.

We leave the circle and enter the library's top floor, take elevators down to a meeting room where, an hour ago, the faculty members met to prepare for the second part of the evening by stacking course syllabi and books on a table. Here the teachers formally introduce their subjects to the students.

Bridget Newell, a trim and poised woman in her forties who is a professor of philosophy and assistant provost of global learning at Westminster College, describes the philosophy section she will teach in the spring as "an exploration of questions." She expresses the hope that the students will realize, by the section's end, that philosophy deals with many ideas that they have thought about, in one way or another, all of their lives.

Hikmet Loe, Venture's instructor in art history, looks quizzically at one listener, then another. She speaks with a directness borne of her northeastern origins, though she has been a Utahn long enough to know, love, and write expertly about western land art. In the circle, she explains that art history is a way of understanding the past that they may have never experienced before. The paintings, sculpture, and architecture they will study provides insights into history and cultures around the world and, perhaps, into themselves.

Associate director at Utah Humanities and an adjunct instructor in writing and literature at Westminster College, Jean Cheney leans from her chair into the conversation, listening intently. A gentle woman in her early sixties, she describes critical writing as a process of discovery, a never-easy journey that clarifies thought and expands understanding. "As writers, you will build connections with the ideas of others," she says, "someone sitting next to you in class or the words of an author who lived two thousand years ago. Often you won't know what you think until you try to write it. There are lots of aha moments ahead for you."

The faculty members speak of the rewards of an enlightened society, based on reason and exploration, and the challenges they include—the language of poetry, the connections among people uncovered through art history, the tragedies and triumphs embodied in American history. We describe the coursework to introduce students to the curriculum but also to let them know that we will be with them as they navigate what is ahead. We know that some of the ideas they will encounter in Venture can unmoor them. Building a community from the very beginning to help them through these encounters and develop new ways of thinking is essential to keep them from feeling adrift.

In the classroom, as we sit in a circle again, a community is already beginning to form. It feels almost tribal. Jeff reads a favorite poem by Naomi Shihab Nye, "My Father and the Fig Tree," and intentionally leaves the last stanza unread.[2] Juanita stares at him. She has been moving her arms ever so slightly to the beat of the poem. She knows this work. She carries poetry in her bones. And when Jeff doesn't complete this poem, she waits.

Toward the end of the evening, she says to Jeff, "I wanted to hear those last lines. I love them."

"So, Juanita, will you bring a copy of the poem next week and read it to the class?" Jeff asks.

"Yes," she replies, "and I will read the whole poem."

For Juanita, it will be poetry. For Kasim, a long way from home, it will be a fig tree tucked inside a poem.

As we learn more about the students we will be teaching, we are already reimagining how we will teach them. We have an unusual number of immigrants and refugees with us this year, and a few are struggling with English. Ahmed smiles broadly. He puts his hand over his heart when he speaks of the opportunity. To his left, Kasim sits in silence. He is still shy, but his eyes examine everything going on around him. It is difficult to guess what he is thinking.

Beside the stack of books students need for the first semester are piles of cobalt blue canvas book bags, emblazoned with "Venture Course in the Humanities" on the side. Toward the end of the evening, as she puts her new books and materials into her blue bag, Ella looks at Jean. "I can't wait to begin," she says, her chin high, eyes bright. She nods as if to say this again, then turns and walks out the door.

NOTES

1.   This is not her real name. Students' names in the text have been changed to protect their identities. We have, however, used real names of students who have submitted their work for various publications, volunteered it for the Venture exhibit, "Transformations through the Humanities," in 2005, or shared it on the Utah Humanities website. Those students who have given us permission to use their poems have their names on the work.

2.   Naomi Shihab Nye, "My Father and the Fig Tree," *19 Varieties of Gazelle: Poems of the Middle East* (New York: Greenwillow Books, 2002), 6.

FROM NEW YORK TO UTAH

JEAN CHENEY

*Not long ago, I had given in to the thought that my life was a waste, pretty
much finished. I had no life. I didn't think I was capable of going to school,
much less ever being a productive or creative human being. Though I know
I have quite a struggle ahead of me, the Venture Course has given me a
sense of capability again, that maybe there is a reason to live. I believe
that it is never too late to be what you could have been.*

—VENTURE COURSE GRADUATE,
FROM AN ANONYMOUS ONLINE SURVEY

THE MEETING

One November morning in 1998, *Harper's* contributing editor and writer Earl
Shorris stood at a podium in a hotel meeting room in Washington, DC. He
had been invited to address a session of the annual conference of the Federation of State Humanities Councils.[1] Organizers of the meeting had asked
him to talk about an experimental humanities program he was running for
poor people at the Roberto Clemente Community Center in New York City.

A short, amiable man in his late sixties, dressed in a dark shirt and sport coat, Shorris soon ignored the microphone. Resting his arm on the podium, he spoke to his audience as if he were at a bar, talking with old friends. "They told me I was crazy trying to teach philosophy to the poor," he said. "It's impossible to teach Socrates to homeless people. The Clemente Course is a nutty idea.'" The conference brochure explained that Clemente was like an open university for people living in poverty, providing an elite Great Books education, taught by college faculty, for people off the street. It met at night twice a week at the Roberto Clemente Community Center in New York City and was based on Petrarch's definition of the humanities from the late Middle Ages: art and literature, moral philosophy, logic. Bard College in upstate New York offered academic credit to those completing the course.

A lover of philosophy since his youth, Shorris had had a brief stint as a bullfighter and a successful career in marketing. For most of his adult life, he had been a novelist and journalist. Throughout his career, he had also been a student of poverty. He wanted to understand its causes and the reasons for its hold on people. His research often led him to the experts—those who were poor or had been poor.

The Clemente Course wasn't his idea. He had been visiting Bedford Hills Correctional Facility for Women in New York, sitting in a circle with inmates discussing family violence and other issues related to poverty. When he asked the woman sitting next to him, Niecie Walker, why people are or stay poor, she replied, "Because we lack the moral life of downtown." Shorris was taken aback. Was she referring to religion? "We don't have plays, or concerts, or lectures," Walker explained. "We don't have these in our lives." "Oh, you mean the humanities?" Shorris asked. "She looked at me as if I were an idiot and said, 'Yeah, Earl, I mean the humanities.'"

Walker's reply hit home. Shorris's life had been shaped by his study of philosophy. He had entered the University of Chicago at thirteen, a highly precocious scholarship kid from El Paso, Texas. At the university, he became immersed in the Great Books curriculum, developed by Robert Maynard Hutchins, and was persuaded by Hutchins's idea that the "best education for the best is the best education for all." After he left Chicago, he served in the military and, eventually—after a career in business—became a journalist and contributing editor to *Harper's*. The magazine often ran his articles about politics and issues related to poverty.

Continuing his conversation with his audience, Shorris described the Clemente Course. Students learn American history, not because it is the most important but because America is where we live, and—to understand the country, its politics and struggles—you need to know its history. In all of the sections of the course, students read primary sources, not textbooks. The Declaration of Independence, Plato's "Allegory of the Cave," Shakespeare's sonnets, Kant's essays all find a place. Students look at slides of art from prehistory to modern times and, when possible, visit museums to see art for themselves. Students sit with the instructor in a circle. There is no podium. There are essays but few tests.

The faculty members teach by posing Socratic questions. The Clemente Course strives to develop reflective thinking and a habit of mind that challenges and questions, instead of accepting "truth" from an authority, whether a teacher or a text. Shorris described Socrates as the founding father of the course because he challenged the prevailing thought of his time and taught critical thinking through dialogue, reasoning, and examining one's thoughts.

Those who taught the Clemente Course, Shorris explained, were his poker-playing buddies. Among them were a Pulitzer Prize–winning historian, a journalist, and a professor at NYU. Some students in that first class had been homeless, addicted to drugs, or recently released from prison. Most were members of ethnic minorities, and none had set foot in a college classroom before this course. "They were wonderful students," Shorris said warmly, as if remembering each one. "They would stand out in the snow and ice after class, still arguing about ideas brought up during their discussions." Although the main goal of the course wasn't to provide a bridge to college but an introduction to a new way of seeing and being in the world, seventeen of the original twenty-three earned certificates, and fourteen earned transferable credits from Bard College. Most of those eventually enrolled in four-year colleges.

By the time Shorris spoke to his DC audience, the Clemente Course had started to spread. State humanities councils in Massachusetts, Washington, and Illinois had initiated courses. He hoped more would come on board.

In Shorris's audience that day were humanities professionals who ran public programs in their respective states. After his talk, they peppered him with questions: "Who is paying for the course? What do students do after graduating if they don't go to college? Why did Bard College agree to offer credit? Why did you choose Petrarch's definition of the humanities?"

Some wondered aloud whether a Clemente course should be part of what a state humanities council did. A free college-level course for people living in poverty brings the humanities into the public sphere in a way, but the audience is small. It differs fundamentally from what state councils usually offer—public lectures, museum exhibits, book discussions in libraries. If the Clemente Course represented public engagement in the humanities, it was on a different scale and, perhaps, had a different purpose.

Others noted that the course accomplished what a lot of humanities councils try to do. It ignited thought and encouraged those disconnected from their communities to engage. It used the humanities to inspire greater reflection. It built a bridge to higher education for people who had been shut out of America's colleges and universities because they were poor and had no idea they belonged there.

I was in the audience that day. New to public humanities work, I had spent my career in college and high school classrooms teaching literature and composition, mostly to privileged white students with backgrounds similar to mine, occasionally to nontraditional adult students in night classes. A recent transplant to Utah, I had joined the staff of the Utah Humanities Council (UHC) looking for fresh ways to use my education and experience. This was my first meeting of state councils. I was sitting beside experienced leaders of humanities programming from around the county, but I was a greenhorn. I was still trying to figure out what state humanities councils were supposed to do.

But from the moment Shorris described what had happened inside that community center in New York City, I was hooked. I wanted to try this. I wanted to bring a Clemente course to Utah. Clemente felt to me like a way of doing something important. At a time when the humanities were being marginalized, Shorris had put them front and center for a group of people who had never known what they were missing.

I started reading more about this odd college course. Once they discovered philosophy and poetry, history and art, Clemente students reported they never wanted to be without them. They suddenly recognized what it felt like to make real choices and know why they were choosing, to have the language to talk about their feelings and ideas, to understand the big stage on which they were living their lives.

Shorris also made me aware of something I hadn't given much thought to. What might someone who had grown up poor and, perhaps, experienced racism and violence do with a humanities education? What profound difference could it make in his or her life? Shorris's experience in New York demonstrated what should be obvious but in many circles is not: because you are poor and undereducated doesn't mean you can't understand and be enriched by the "best which has been thought and said," as Matthew Arnold put it.[2] Sophocles, Socrates, and Shakespeare belong to former addicts and prison inmates. The work of Adrienne Rich, Sandra Cisneros, Richard Rodriguez, and James Baldwin could be lifelines for those struggling to claim their identities in a society that had demeaned them.

As Shorris set out to prove, study of the humanities thrives quite well outside ivy-covered walls. He called this kind of study the ultimate "practical education," not because it leads to a well-paying job but because it can help shape a well-lived life. Learning how to read closely and question teaches you not to react but to analyze, not to acquiesce—or fight—but to think and judge for yourself. More than two thousand years ago, Epictetus didn't mince words: "Only the educated are free."

In "As a Weapon in the Hands of the Restless Poor," Shorris notes that he learned much about poverty in America through listening to more than six hundred poor people tell their stories. From these conversations, he came to understand that people living in poverty are surrounded by forces they have little control over—racism, poor schools, dilapidated housing, ugliness, noise, unfair landlords, illness, violence.[3] These forces keep them from being "political," that is, engaging in "activity with other people at every level, from the family to the neighborhood to the broader community to the city-state."[4] This absence of a political life, he concluded, keeps poor people caught within this "surround of force."

In creating the first Clemente Course, Shorris was essentially making a wager: if they study the humanities, people living in poverty can learn to respond differently to the conditions bearing down on their lives. If they have teachers who invite them into the world of great thinkers, they will recognize philosophy speaks to *them* and develop their voices to speak back. If they discover a demythologized America through primary historical documents and the core ideas and ideals of its founders, they can be emboldened to hold their country more accountable to the truths it has proclaimed and the philosophy of its founding.

Socrates's insistence that he knew nothing for sure and that questioning was the only way to discover how to live and what was true would introduce powerful ways of thinking to students who felt trapped by a society that oppressed them. Asking fundamental questions could lead them out of the dead ends many felt their lives had become. This was the heart of Shorris's wager.

Although it was not part of Shorris's story that morning, the educational model animating Clemente actually has a long history. Generations earlier, Columbia University's John Erskine, a professor of literature, irked his colleagues by proposing the "democratization" of the classics.[5] The world's great literature should be taught to all undergraduates, he argued, rather than remain treasures savored only by the budding literati in humanities departments. Students of psychology, physics, or engineering should read and benefit from the classics, too. When his detractors argued that language barriers made his plan impossible for all but a few, Erskine proposed using English translations of novels such as Tolstoy's *War and Peace*. In 1920—over the strenuous objections of many classicists and other humanities professors—Columbia's faculty adopted the general honors course Erskine had initiated as a requirement for graduation. Although it takes the idea much further—outside the academy—Earl Shorris's "riches for the poor" Clemente Course is a logical extension of Erskine's pioneering reform.

But hadn't these students "studied the humanities" in high school? Yes—and no. As taught in poor neighborhood schools, the humanities leave much to be desired (with some notable exceptions). "Language arts" is often limited to grammar study or work sheets that have to be completed. History is comprised mostly of memorizing who won battles and elections. It is seldom presented as a mighty struggle of ideas or the story of exploitation and domination. Philosophy and art history are often not even included in the curriculum.

I imagined that teaching the Clemente Course would affect everyone involved. We might discover, for the first time, what the humanities could really do. I had witnessed such moments in the classroom. It's often said, by defenders of the humanities, that studying literature connects people with what it means to be human. But it also connects people who differ from one another because of skin color, eye shape, language, gender, or the size of their bank accounts. People profoundly separated by their experience get a glimpse of each other's worlds.

While reading and discussing Ralph Ellison's *Invisible Man,* for example, I have seen white students recoil at the ugly racism. They may have studied facts about slavery and the civil rights movement in history class, but the racism depicted in the novel churns their guts, forcing them to look away from the page. Reading about the humiliation that the young narrator in "Battle Royal" suffers, and then must accept if he is to "get ahead," white students inch closer to knowing truths about an America they do not want to see. These are truths that black students may know all too well but have never talked about with white classmates.

Connections made through works as powerful as *Invisible Man* are not inevitable and never complete. Many issues complicate the ability of students to empathize with one another.[6] But stories and poetry can emit an electric current of understanding that readers do not forget.

In Langston Hughes's "Theme for English B," the narrator writes, "Sometimes perhaps you don't want to be a part of me./Nor do I often want to be a part of you./But we are, that's true!" He continues wryly, "As I learn from you,/I guess you learn from me—/although you're older—and white—/and somewhat more free."[7] The writer understandably resents the unequal worlds "you" and "I" inhabit. But he may underestimate how much those who are "older and white and somewhat more free" need to learn from him if we're ever to dismantle together the edifices of racism, classicism, and sexism in America.

After leaving the conference in DC and returning to Utah, I soon learned that between the wish and its fulfillment falls the budget. UHC is a well-run organization with carefully planned programs and managed finances. There was no money to start a Clemente course. We would need $40,000–$50,000 to cover child care, books, transportation, meeting space, and stipends for five faculty members and the site director.

Finding the money wasn't the only issue. If we didn't want to partner with Bard College—because of its distant location and lack of recognition by many Utah residents—we needed to convince a local academic partner to provide credit. We needed to identify a strong faculty, willing to teach for a modest stipend. We needed walls, a centrally located place on a mass transit line to hold classes. And we needed to learn how to recruit eligible students, people living on very low incomes without access to higher education but with the courage and willingness to commit to a rigorous academic schedule.

All of this coordination and direction would take time. I had other responsibilities, and there was no money to hire someone to take them over. I read Shorris's book, *Riches for the Poor,* then put the book and my dream for the course on the shelf.

THE ANGEL

Five years later, in the spring of 2003, an old friend and frequent donor to UHC dropped by our office. She had read about the Clemente Course in the *Los Angeles Times.* A strong believer in broadening educational opportunities, she asked a simple question: "Would UHC be interested in starting a Clemente course?" If so, she could connect us with a funding source. They might be willing to pay for a pilot program.

Executive Director Cynthia Buckingham and I spent little time answering her. In the Clemente Course, we saw a chance to broaden our audience beyond those whose lives were already enriched by the humanities: middle-aged, college-educated, mostly white people. We had a hard time serving diverse audiences with our current programs, especially people in poverty. Some rural audiences and small-town residents, many of whom were far from wealthy, took advantage of our reading groups and museum programs, but they usually had books and discussions in their lives already. In spite of limited opportunities available to them, they were not the "poor" that Niecie Walker and Earl Shorris had talked about.

Residents from the west side of Salt Lake City, on the other hand, where many minorities and refugees lived and the median annual income in 2005 was less than $20,000, rarely knew about us or came to our programs. The same was true in Utah's smaller cities—Ogden, Logan, Cedar City. Clemente would offer a humanities program to these audiences and also introduce other opportunities through UHC. The Clemente Course could be half program, half outreach. "Yes!" we said to our angel. "We will draft a plan."

Alternative Visions, a fund of the Chicago Community Trust, agreed to the plan we outlined, providing support for six months to develop the course and sufficient money for a pilot program. After receiving this commitment, I set to work. I knew from the beginning that we would develop a western version of the Clemente Course. We would be heavily indebted to the model but modify it for Utah soil.

I imagined, for example, that the experienced professors we wanted to attract might not want to limit readings to the Great Books curriculum. More likely, they would draw from their years in the classroom to choose texts from a wide range of cultural sources and periods. Students who enrolled in our course might come from the large immigrant and refugee population here. We have families living on very low incomes from all over the world. Some Great Books would be included, especially Greek philosophers for their influence on Western thought, and we would certainly teach seminal documents from American history, but there would be modern texts, too, from America and many other cultures. In the spirit of America's humanities councils, a loose federation of independent organizations, UHC would adopt, adapt, and innovate this program that brought the humanities into the street.

THE FACULTY

I started with what I knew would make or break the course—the faculty. Given the unique teaching challenge that the Clemente Course represented, I was unsure how to go about recruiting them. Keeping in mind Shorris's eventual experience in New York with the first Clemente Course (as it turned out, not all of those brilliant poker buddies taught well), I knew the most important qualities in the Venture teachers had to be passion for their disciplines and the ability to engage the wide variety of adults brave enough to sign up for the course. I asked people I knew—some who were professors—to recommend outstanding colleagues in the humanities. I relied on reputation. One by one, I interviewed faculty members to teach philosophy, literature, American history, and art history. We discussed the course and how to adapt it to Utah and their teaching interests. I liked each of them, and not one turned down the offer to join the team.

To understand this course and what should happen in it, I needed to be one of the faculty members, I told myself. I should teach the writing segment. Truthfully I simply wanted to experience students who might never have had the chance to read serious literature, study the history that had shaped their world, or share their stories. How would these adult students respond to the essayists I loved, such as Emerson, Thoreau, Twain or Orwell, Baldwin, Sanders, Rodriguez, Rich, or Anzaldúa? What would they choose to write about? I wanted to join this band of teachers and ride this train.

This same team taught together for seven years until career and life changes intervened. We became close friends who laughed, argued, ate, and drank together. We often said we were lucky to have found each other. But it wasn't really luck. We were drawn by the same star. Each of us wanted to share our academic passions with people who lacked access to higher education and provide a chance for them to develop the power of their minds. We wanted to offer a safe space for them to reflect about their lives and to use this humanities study to help them gain more control over their futures. And we wanted to learn from them; we knew they had much to teach us.

Some years ago, four of us decided we wanted to share what we had experienced in a book in the hope that more Clemente courses like Venture could grow in U.S. communities. It's a story we believe needs to be told. Earl Shorris has written a book about starting the first Clemente Course and another about student experiences in Clemente courses around the world, but little has been written about starting a course modeled on Clemente—and what to expect if you do.[8]

We've been motivated by another hope. As many have noted, the humanities have come to be regarded as dispensable subjects, nice to have if you can afford to indulge in them. What we learn through philosophy and the history of art is not considered as critical as what we can do with computers and calculus.[9]

We are convinced such thinking misunderstands the ways a humanities education prepares one for life. It presents a false choice. A city planner with no appreciation for history is not someone we want designing our cities. A doctor who has never developed the habit of listening carefully is not someone we want caring for us. A legislator who has never studied ethics or realized that there can be two legitimate, if conflicting, points of view is not someone we want making our laws.

Teaching in Venture has convinced us that everyone needs the humanities. Whether they continue in college or not, become teachers or store managers, lawyers or plumbers, studying the humanities gives adults a fuller sense of their humanity and the many ways they belong to the motley, magnificent, miserable lot that is the human race. They come to understand that Frederick Douglass speaks to them, matters to them, whatever their skin color or life experience may be. The music and wisdom in Shakespeare's sonnets belong to them; the truths in the Declaration of Independence are ones they can claim.

These are not small realizations. They lead to a greater ability to reason and reflect, and these build people's confidence as thinkers and writers. Studying the humanities can lead to the biggest change of all: the ability to become "the people they always wanted to be" and help those around them, especially their children, do the same. We have always known that the humanities aren't peripheral to an education; they are its heart.

NOTES

1. The Federation of State Humanities Councils is a membership organization comprised of councils from all fifty U.S. states, Puerto Rico, Guam, and the Marianna Islands. The federation holds an annual conference for members to share ideas, hear guest speakers, and benefit from the work of their peers. State humanities councils receive funding from the National Endowment for the Humanities, foundations, corporations, and individuals. They are independent, nonprofit organizations, not government agencies.

2. Matthew Arnold, preface to *Culture and Anarchy: An Essay in Political and Social Criticism*, viii, https://ia801404.us.archive.org/1/items/cultureandanarcooarnogoog/cultureandanarcooarnogoog.pdf.

3. Earl Shorris, "On the Uses of a Liberal Education: II. As a Weapon in the Hands of the Restless Poor," *Harper's*, September 1997, 50–59.

4. Ibid., 50.

5. John Erskine, *The Moral Obligation to Be Intelligent and Other Essays* (New York: Duffield and Company, 1915).

6. For a fuller discussion of the ways literature helps develop empathy, see Martha Nussbaum, *Poetic Justice: The Literary Imagination and Public Life* (Boston: Beacon Press, 1995), 5.

7. Langston Hughes, "Theme for English B," in *The Norton Anthology of Modern Poetry*, ed. Richard Ellmann and Robert O'Clair, 640–41. (New York: W. W. Norton & Company, 1973).

8. Earl Shorris, *The Art of Freedom: Teaching the Humanities to the Poor* (New York: W. W. Norton & Company, 2013). This volume was published posthumously after Shorris's death in 2012. It includes interviews with Venture students that Shorris conducted during his visit to Utah in 2011.

9. For a recent expression of this view, see Patricia Cohen, "A Rising Call to Promote STEM Education and Cut Liberal Arts Funding," *New York Times*, February 21, 2016, http://www.nytimes.com/2016/02/22/business/a-rising-call-to-promote-stem-education-and-cut-liberal-arts-funding.html?_r=0.

CREATING VENTURE

JEAN CHENEY

There is truth in the statement, "It is important in life to know when your cue comes." But it is more important to have the courage to create your own cues to improve your job prospects or make your neighborhood a better place. The sooner you accept that truth, the sooner you accept responsibility for your own life.

—MARIA JUAREZ, *VENTURE GRADUATION SPEECH, 2007*

From the beginning, the Venture Course was based on the original, 1995 model of a Clemente Course but with differences. To start, we decided against using the Clemente name. It made sense in New York City, where the Roberto Clemente Community Center is known, but not in Utah. And we wanted to go our own way in choosing a curriculum. The five subjects struck us as right. They offered enough breadth to appeal to and inform students and enough time—eleven two-hour class meetings each—to provide some depth. Teaching using Socratic dialogue wasn't an issue. All of us employed purposeful, yet open-ended, discussion, rather than lectures, using questions to probe and engage students. We already assigned writing, rather than tests, as evidence of learning.

But we wanted to depart from the Great Books approach Shorris used to include more contemporary authors from diverse cultures, and, most of all, we wanted direction over the way the course evolved. Shorris had developed a brilliant idea, but we wanted to shape it to fit our situation and the needs of the people who would become our students. The name "Venture" fit what we aimed to do. Given the pressures they lived with every day, it took courage for students to sign up to study subjects whose very names intimidated them. Most adults with little exposure to higher education find the study of philosophy, art history, and critical writing foreign and may have negative memories about studying American history and literature. Venture also suggested their expectation. You venture because you hope to gain something, unknowable in the beginning, elusive even, but promising.

It wasn't just the students who would be venturing. As teachers, we were testing and experimenting, exploring what the humanities could do outside academia with students who lived difficult lives and whose preparation for the rigors of academic study was modest, at best, but whose hunger for something they couldn't name was intense. Would our privileged backgrounds make connecting with Venture students difficult? Would we need to change the way we teach? What texts and topics would resonate the most with these untraditional students? We didn't know the answers to these questions, but we were eager to find out.

OUR ACADEMIC PARTNER

Seeking an academic partner close to home, we approached officials at the University of Utah with the Venture idea, described the program with great enthusiasm, and promised initial funding to get it off the ground. The university was a natural fit. A quick ride on light rail from downtown Salt Lake City, the U of U is the largest academic institution in the state. Since it is a commuter school with many nontraditional students and a strong connection to the community through its sports, arts, and volunteer programs, partnering with it made sense. We talked to deans and faculty members who were attracted to the concept.

Then came the roadblocks. Because it is a public university, the course needed to be open to all students, we were told; we couldn't limit it to those living on low incomes. And how would credit be assigned? The individual departments needed to weigh in. That meant having curriculum approved. How could a University of Utah course be taught by non-University of Utah faculty? We would have to limit our teachers to those already on the faculty, as either full time or adjuncts, or gain departmental approval.

We were sinking into a quagmire. If the course were approved, it would take months, maybe years, to get it off the ground, and we would lose any possibility for control over faculty, curriculum, and course management.

Most of the time, Mary Jane Chase, dean of the School of Arts and Sciences at Westminster College in 2004, looks as if she has just heard a good joke.[1] In her view, the world, including the fine small college where she teaches, is an entertaining place, full of frailty and possibility. With impressive academic credentials—a doctorate in history from Stanford and a book about Renaissance France—she had the reputation of being a problem solver with a lightning-quick mind. She led the School of Arts and Sciences with wisdom and humor.

I visited Mary Jane—the name she prefers to be called—in her office on campus. I knew her from my years as an adjunct teacher in the English Department. She cleared a space for us at a small round table stacked with papers and books. "There's a new course that UHC wants to start, and we're looking for an academic partner," I began. I was eager for Mary Jane to realize the uniqueness of our endeavor and its advantages to the college. "These would be students who would probably never find their way to Westminster," I continued. "But they might, through this course. It could help the college in its efforts to reach nontraditional students and bridge the 'gown/town' divide."

I should have known that Mary Jane wouldn't need the pitch. She immediately saw the course more broadly: "Whether these students find their way here or not, this course is important," she said. "The humanities are core. Everyone should have access to them. They can change lives."

I described the structure of the course: the sections were taught over two semesters, and a Westminster philosophy professor, Bridget Newell, had already expressed interest in teaching. Mary Jane looked up from the notes she was writing on a yellow pad. "Bridget would be great," she said. "Who else?"

"There would be three professors from the University of Utah in addition to Bridget, all experienced teachers. And me. I really want to do this."

"Sounds like a good group. I think we could offer credit. Let me check with the provost." Venture had found its academic partner—in less than five minutes.

The provost agreed with the dean's recommendation. With credit coming from Westminster, Venture immediately acquired some cachet. The college was widely respected in Utah and the Mountain West for its undergraduate teaching and master's degrees in education, business, and nursing. It was experiencing rapid growth with a new library, new residence halls, and plans for a new science center. More relevant to Venture, it had recently made a commitment to increasing the diversity of its student body, and it regularly invited the Salt Lake community to hear the writers and thinkers hosted on campus speak about issues related to the divides created by race, gender, and class. Westminster was also expanding its Center for Civic Engagement to forge connections between students and immigrant and refugee communities in Salt Lake City.

But as a private college, Westminster was also very expensive; its annual tuition exceeded $20,000 in 2004. If they wanted to continue their education there, Venture students would not be able to afford even a semester unless they received full scholarships. We thought it was worth a gamble, though, to partner with this small liberal-arts college. It had people like Mary Jane who believed deeply in the value of the humanities for everyone, and the provost and president supported our efforts. The general education credits that Venture students earned from Westminster would be transferrable.

Westminster came on board that first year offering credit and a student ID card, enabling students to ride the bus or light rail and use the library and other campus facilities. It invited students to receptions and lectures and provided a beautiful auditorium for Venture's graduation ceremony. Over the years, Westminster has increased its support. It now assumes the majority of the cost of the course.

Since the partnership began, Venture alumni have attended and won scholarships from Westminster. One was a McNair scholar who continued on to graduate school. But—as Mary Jane saw immediately in 2004—the partnership was not intended primarily to attract students. Supporting the Venture Course would help the college make a statement to the community about the power of the liberal arts outside its walls. Westminster was beginning to welcome more diverse students to its campus, but it also thought its campus should extend into the community.

OUR HOME

Now for Venture's walls. Where should we teach this course? Like many American cities, Salt Lake is divided geographically by income and ethnicity. Most people of color and those with low incomes reside in neighborhoods on the west side of the Salt Lake Valley. Wealthy neighborhoods cluster along the east side benches of the Wasatch Mountains. We decided not to hold classes at Westminster College, which is perched on one of those benches, far from the neighborhoods where we imagined many of our potential students lived. They could reach Westminster by public transportation, but it would be a long commute, and buses did not run after eight o'clock. Finally, the college had no day-care facility.

When you walk into Horizonte Instruction and Training Center on Main Street in the heart of downtown Salt Lake City, you feel a little as if you have just entered a mini United Nations. Bright, colorful flags from countries around the world hang along the bannisters of the airy, five-story atrium. Middle-aged, dark-skinned men, speaking Arabic, are conversing as they enter the elevator. Two Latinas are coming down the stairs, speaking Spanish. In the foyer, teenage mothers hold the hands of toddlers as they walk toward a door marked Day Care. Horizonte is Salt Lake City's "alternative" high school, a home for pregnant girls who have dropped out of school, teens who have flunked out because of bad behavior or failing grades, and adult immigrants and refugees who want to learn English. It is also a night school for working adults returning to earn their GEDs.

On a wall on the fourth floor is an enormous, floor-to-ceiling painting of a weeping Virgin Mary, painted in brilliant colors by Ruby Chacon, a gifted Chicana artist with deep family roots in Utah. James Andersen, Horizonte's principal for more than twenty years, greets a group of Venture faculty members in front of this painting. Soon after shaking hands, he says, "It may seem like a small thing, but nowhere is there a mark of graffiti on the walls or a scrap of paper on the floor here. There never has been, not since the school started. Our students take pride in their school."

We look around. Students look happy, purposeful. They cluster in small groups, talking. No one wanders through the halls. In fact, there are no halls—all doors open to a walkway around the atrium, which is full of light. The east side of the building is a glass wall facing the majestic Wasatch Mountains. On Horizonte's sign outside the school is its slogan: "As far as the eye can see, as far as the mind can reach."

Andersen embraced Venture from the beginning. "The course will be consistent with what we do here," he said. "I'll show you our library on the fourth floor. You could hold classes there. There's a day-care center your students can use on the first floor, just inside the door." He welcomed the chance to reach more adults with educational programming without having to expand his faculty. That helped him boost numbers and use facilities that weren't occupied during the evening. The school was located on a main transportation route, close to where our students probably lived. We had found Venture's home.

OUR STUDENTS

From the beginning of the Venture experience, we were also different from the original Clemente Course in the students we attracted and the way we thought about them. Earl Shorris described Clemente students as "the poor." He focused on the similarities in the lives of these poor, making many generalizations about them. They were surrounded by forces they had little control over. They did not have a voice in the political system, nor did they have the tools or experience to reflect on their lives. They were victims of racism and classism. They had experienced all the ways that poverty demeans and depresses the human spirit.

As we began recruiting—through libraries, laundromats, agencies serving those living on low incomes, Head Start Centers, and churches—and met the first class of Venture students, we realized that calling them the "poor" was an incomplete and misleading characterization. Yes, the students had low incomes, some very low by American (and federal government) standards. Living on a low income (no more than 50 percent above the federal poverty level) was a requirement for the course. But most had jobs, and some were living a fairly stable, modest life. Some had been homeless, but others had secure homes. A few had been in prison; others had volunteered in their communities. A large number, to our surprise, had experienced an illness or accident, severely limiting their opportunities. Many had had few chances to get a decent education because of the neighborhoods where they grew up, the parents they never had, and/or the racism they encountered. A few had experienced severe discrimination because they were female in patriarchal cultures or their sexual orientation ostracized them in religiously orthodox societies.

Some came from loving families; others had oppressive, cruel parents. Some of our students were refugees who had been living middle-class or fairly comfortable lives in their home countries but faced social and economic barriers caused by language and their lack of academic credentials in the United States. We had students recovering from drug addictions, suffering from lupus, or surviving cancer. Our students were hard to characterize. Most lived hard lives, but they did not fit easily into a specific category. We could not describe them as "the poor."

OUR CURRICULUM

As with the original Clemente Course, we wanted Venture to include sections in the five subjects Petrarch believed comprised the humanities: literature, philosophy, art, history, and logic—or critical writing and thinking. These subjects struck us as comprehensive enough to introduce a range of humanistic ways of thinking and develop students' ability to question, analyze, synthesize, and debate. They would empower students as thinkers.

With eleven class meetings available for each subject—a total of fifty-five classes in all—we had to decide how to divide them over an academic year. It made sense to begin with the subjects we thought might be most approachable for students: literature and art history. We assumed that most of our students would be accustomed to story and poetry or song in the culture where they had grown up. We hoped they would respond to art as a nonverbal language and be intrigued by the insights into history it provided. The fall semester would be followed by philosophy and American history in the spring, potentially more challenging subjects with longer reading assignments, especially if they were structured the way we wanted to teach them, focusing on big ideas and using primary texts.

We weren't sure where to place the writing section. We knew all of the sections would assign writing, and we wanted the writing class to help students meet these challenges. We also imagined that critical writing would be difficult for the students. Beyond some basic instruction in high school, we couldn't assume our students had ever studied writing or written essays. Although the other four sections would assign writing as a way to learn and demonstrate learning, the writing section would concentrate on teaching writing as a process and skill. It would use essays from a wide variety of writers as models. We decided that it would be best to teach writing over the course of the two semesters, meeting the same number of times as the other sections with the meetings further apart, to give students more time to digest what they were learning and help them complete assignments.

Thus, we began the course with literature and art history in the fall, trying to engage students with creative expressions of what it means to be human. Six classes of the writing section were scheduled in the fall, followed by five in the spring, which spread out both the instruction and the chance to practice. Philosophy and American history followed in the spring, introducing students to big questions: What can we know, and how can we know it? What are the tenets of American democracy, and what are its core beliefs? How has America fulfilled and betrayed those tenets and beliefs over its four-hundred-year history?

It isn't a perfect structure. Every year it feels as if there is too little time to do what we have planned. We have scaled back ambitious syllabi in favor of emphasizing the processes of reading, writing, and thinking. We had to address and adjust concerns about how well we were covering our disciplines to focus more on what the students were learning. Our emphasis shifted from introducing students to the major aspects of our subject areas to connecting their lives to the ideas, art, and texts we were discussing.

Every year we include classical and contemporary stories and poetry from a variety of cultures. Mary Oliver's poem "The Journey" is taught in the very beginning of the literature section because it describes—in an accessible, powerful way—an anguish many of our students know well. Pablo Neruda, Derek Wolcott, Sappho, Shakespeare, Sandra Cisneros, Robert Hayden, and Naomi Shihab Nye have all found a place in that class. Art history moves from prehistory through the Greeks and Romans, the Renaissance, and into the modern period. In philosophy, students always read Plato's "Allegory of the Cave" and some moral philosophy but also a mix of contemporary philosophers. In American history, students rely on primary sources, as the original Clemente Course did, including the Declaration of Independence, the Bill of Rights, the Declaration of Sentiments and Resolutions from Seneca Falls, and Martin Luther King Jr.'s "Letter from Birmingham Jail." In critical writing, students sometimes read *Antigone* but always study classic and contemporary essayists for models of the form.

It never seems enough. The list of readings and art could be twice as long. We console ourselves by remembering Venture is only meant to be a beginning. We've learned that we can't totally satisfy the desire for learning that our students bring with them, but we can begin.

After we developed this curriculum and began teaching, we realized that we had sharply different teaching styles and, to some degree, philosophies. Like the history behind the idea of "Great Books for all," these different and approaches also have a history. The generative reform era in college teaching that surrounded World War I revealed a cleavage that Shorris did not explicitly recognize, yet was manifested quite naturally in teaching the Clemente curriculum. Should course content drive teaching, as Shorris, John Erskine, and Robert Hutchins believed, or should spontaneity and exploration prompt classroom dynamics, as philosopher John Dewey and psychologist Howard Warren thought? If something has to give—and it usually does—will it be the structured subject matter or the unpredictable processes through which students and teachers discover new knowledge?

We jumped into our Venture teaching paying little attention to this dichotomy but soon found that we spanned the range from Dewey to Hutchins. Jeff Metcalf teaches literature by focusing on students' joy and their discovery of personal meaning, which is as important to him as the works they read. On the Hutchins side of the spectrum, Hikmet Loe and Bridget Newell pay more attention to the principles of philosophy and art history and choose classical texts and art, while also incorporating contemporary works and responding to students' needs and interests. Jack Newell strikes a balance between the importance of students knowing the primary documents and issues in American history and their ability to shape classroom conversations that illuminate their personal struggles with the issues we face now.

Because teaching writing is chiefly developing a skill, Jean Cheney's task is a bit different, but her segment of the course bends toward Dewey because she reacts spontaneously to what occurs in the classroom, although she also includes classical essays and texts as writing models and teaches the steps of the "writing process" that is taught in most college classrooms.

Every year students respond well to the range of instruction and seem to respect the differences in our teaching philosophies. Clearly the freedom we have to "be ourselves" in the classroom strengthens what each of us offers. Our mutual responsibilities to provide both sound content and a dynamic classroom environment keep each of us within range of the others.

OUR ADMINISTRATION

In the beginning, one of our five faculty members also served as the site director. She publicized the course in the spring; recruited students, interviewed them, and arranged for their enrollment at Westminster; ordered books for the faculty members; planned fall orientation; attended every class; helped with video equipment; and ensured teachers had the supplies they needed during class. A large part of her time was spent mentoring students as they began to adjust—or not adjust—to the expectations of the course. When students had to be absent, they called her, and she was the liaison among the students, our home school (Horizonte Instruction and Training Center), and Westminster College. In the spring, she supported students as they planned their graduation ceremony.

Funding for the course originally came from UHC with Westminster College contributing college credit and a student ID card, and Horizonte providing the meeting space. The course was, in effect, a program of all three of these partners but was not directed by any one of them.

Over time, Westminster College increased its support and now contributes the majority of the funding. The Venture Course is still a largely independent organization, however. Unconcerned about bureaucracies or competition with peers and blessed with intimacy, we have developed our own curriculum, teaching methods, and ways to solve problems. As a faculty, we are united and guided by our pursuit of one goal: to create the best education that we possibly can for a group of adults eager to improve their lives. We have answered only to Venture's mission and our students, aware that for many of them, perhaps most of them, this may be their last and best chance to have a formal education in the humanities and become the —people they very much want to be. We have sometimes disagreed about what that best education is exactly, but we have resolved those disagreements, recognizing that what we teach and how we teach can have wide margins.

CRITIQUES OF THE CLEMENTE COURSE

Over the years, we have become aware of critiques of the Clemente model and have shared some of these opinions but disagreed with others. Like Jeanne M. Connell, we think the course enables students to see their lives differently and take on new challenges, including continuing with higher education.[2] We agree with Connell that Shorris did not prove that it was the classically inspired humanities curriculum that produced these changes. We've seen similar results to the ones he cited using a much more diverse set of readings, both contemporary and classic.

Shorris often claimed Socrates and the Socratic method were the beating heart of the Clemente Course because reading Socrates and engaging in guided questioning were essential for empowering students to lead a better life. But James Scott Johnston and Timothy L. Simpson argue that Shorris's conception focuses on "Socrates the dialogician, Socrates the gadfly, Socrates the democrat" and doesn't emphasize Socrates the truth seeker nearly enough.[3] They argue that omitting the focus on truth seeking diminishes the potential for poor people to use the skills and methods they can learn from him to seek justice. This leaves them without "the means to grasp a standard of justice from which they can change the game."[4]

In Venture, as in most Clemente courses, we use dialogue to develop critical thinking, reflection, and analytical skills so that students find their own truths. These can and do help students come to a clearer understanding of justice, which can influence their social, political, and personal behavior or "change the game," as Johnston and Simpson put it.

Jennifer Ng argues that Shorris does not fully acknowledge the structural aspects of poverty and places too much responsibility on poor people to change their behavior without requiring that the privileged or affluent do the same.[5] Shorris did not state explicitly enough that there need to be many structural changes in education and society to address poverty, she states. Further, she notes that the Clemente Course is designed for only *some* poor people—those who meet the specific criteria to attend the class (those who can read at a certain level and commit to attending class two nights a week for many months). This limits the ability of the Clemente Course to remedy poverty, in her view.

Our response to Ng is, in short, "of course." The Clemente Course cannot address the needs of all people living in poverty, nor all of the reasons why people are poor. Its success is in empowering students to make new choices that *they want to make* and enriching their lives, but it does not guarantee they can reach all of their goals nor necessarily raise their incomes. There are enormous obstacles to getting ahead in America, including the cost of higher education and the barriers encountered by adults with families who wish to continue their learning. But we believe that the success of the Venture Course—as well as Clemente courses elsewhere—in empowering adults to make positive changes in their lives should convince anyone in education that the humanities are critical to helping people in poverty. Are these courses the grand answer to poverty in America? Obviously not. Do they indicate what we need to be doing in designing curricula and programs that make a difference in the lives of people who are poor? Indeed, yes!

OUR COMMUNITY

As conceived originally, the Clemente Course saw scholars and experts sharing the treasures of the Western world with those who had never known them, giving "riches to the poor," in Shorris's words, sharing the wealth that only those with elite educations could access. Teachers, through the privilege of their experience and education, introduced the humanities to those who had been shut out of the world of the classics and great ideas.

Although we did not consciously plan it, we realized almost immediately that we were deviating from this model. We watched as three learning communities formed in Venture: the one our students created, the one the faculty shaped among ourselves, and the one fashioned by the students and faculty together.

Almost from the beginning, our students formed a community in the classroom. They brought food to share, wept at each other's stories, supported each other during the inevitable slumps, and encouraged their fellow students to write outstanding poems and papers. Their caring for each other affected all of us deeply and helped shape the Venture experience. But they were also intellectual cocreators of course content, actively participating and helping to guide the conversation. Their interests and needs helped us know where to focus and when to let go.

The faculty formed a community among its members, too, talking about what and why we taught what we did, sharing stories from our lives and our teaching, disagreeing over issues, and always finding ways to resolve our differences. Many Saturday mornings found us commandeering a battered oak table at the Salt Lake Roasting Company, a local café and hangout, where we met to thrash through problems or brainstorm ideas.

The best moments, though, resulted when these two learning communities came together in the classroom. At those moments, why we were there became palpable to everyone. It could happen during the sharing of a poem that silenced all conversation, the words running like a dark river through the quiet. Or when a student said, "I've been in that cave" after reading Plato, then told her story to her fellow travelers, who had also left lives obscured by shadows and illusions. Or it could happen when a student expressed, in a voice that was suddenly sure, his belief that Martin Luther King Jr. had defeated the assassin's bullet with words, just words on a page, the same words that had now changed this student's life.

These are the magical, almost sacred times in Venture. In these moments, it never seems as if we are giving riches to the poor. We are at the same table, feasting together.

NOTES

1. Mary Jane Chase was dean of the School of Arts and Sciences at Westminster College in 2004, when the idea of Venture was broached. Lance Newman is the current dean.
2. Jeanne M. Connell, "Can Those Who Live in Poverty Find Liberation through the Humanities? Or Is This Just a New Romance with an Old Model?" *Educational Studies* 39, no. 1 (February 2006): 15–26.
3. James Scott Johnston and Timothy L. Simpson, "The Use of Socrates: Earl Shorris and the Quest for Political Emancipation through the Humanities," *Educational Studies* 39, no 1 (February 2006): 29.
4. Ibid., 38.
5. Jennifer Ng, "Antipoverty Policy Perspectives: A Historical Examination of the Transference of Social Scientific Thought and a Situated Critique of the Clemente Course," *Educational Studies* 39, no. 1 (February 2006): 41–60.

3

LITERATURE

Improvisation

JEFF METCALF

The poet can contribute toward understanding between peoples. . . . I stand before you, not on my own merits, but as a symbol, for a time, of the significance of poetry.

—T. S. ELIOT, "NOBEL BANQUET SPEECH," 1948

Eleven years ago, at the end of my first literature class for the Venture Course, I was visiting with students outside Horizonte as they slowly drifted off to catch the bus or light rail to head home. One of our students, a middle-aged woman who had been on the edge of the conversation, approached me.

"How did you like the first night?" I asked.

She thought for a moment. "It made me hungry. I've got a hunger."

I was not sure what she meant. "There are several community services that might be able to help out."

She laughed. "It is not about food. I've got a hunger that can't be banished with bacon and beans. It's a hunger to learn."

She gave me my first lesson in the Venture Course. There would be many more.

The literature class sets the Venture program in motion. Since the course begins with this section, I feel a tremendous responsibility to make the students feel comfortable in this new environment.

When students enter class the first night, they are nervous, uncertain. For those who missed the orientation or were overwhelmed by all that happened that night, I take time to explain how the course works. When we've settled in a bit, I have them reintroduce themselves. The students are much more relaxed this time around and listen carefully as each classmate tells his or her story. Several students nod their heads when others talk about the importance of using education to better their lives and be good role models for their children.

I introduce two undergraduate English teaching majors who have joined us from the University of Utah, Beth Snow and Taylor Christiansen. I've invited Beth and Taylor to the Venture Course to fulfill their service-learning requirement at the university with me. Both took courses I taught the previous year, and I liked their restlessness and the way they challenged their peers and the public-school system. I wanted them to see a different teaching design and hoped the experience might, in some way, transform their collective frustration with public education into action that could change it.

Beth and Taylor discuss their reasons for wanting to teach and how much they want to improve public schools. The Venture students applaud.

I am discussing the works we will be reading when Olga interrupts. "Why did *you* want to be a teacher?"

"Ah," I say. "That is a story." I describe my checkered journey through school and the way a single teacher changed the course of my life. I reiterate the importance of education and promise we will do our very best to support the students on this journey. I speak of my love for the craft of teaching and that I think engagement with my students over many years has kept me alive.

When I open the floor for questions, the students ask some personal ones. Atiyah, a middle-aged woman from the previous Venture class, who had to drop the course to help her family and has returned to complete the first semester, asks if I still love to cook. When I tell her that cooking has been keeping me sane and, lately, I have been preparing Middle Eastern food in a tagine, she covers her mouth and laughs. "Does your family like this food?"

"Yes," I assure her. "I am still learning, but none of them has died so far. I have a brave family."

I tell the class that I've been trying to duplicate a particular flatbread I grew up eating as a small boy when we lived in Saudi Arabia. I failed miserably. Ahmed, a thoughtful man who spoke emotionally earlier in the evening about being in the Venture Course, smiles and asks if I learned to speak any Arabic. I answer him with the few Arabic words I know, "Yes, very little, but I like the language." A smile crosses his face.

"We call the bread *khoubz*," I say. Ahmed nods.

When I was a child, my family moved around a great deal, I continue, and I spent ten years living in foreign countries. I feel fortunate to have had this opportunity. My own family—my wife, our two children, and I—have traveled to many countries together. We love experiencing other cultures, I explain.

Suddenly, I realize that the accidental mention of a simple flatbread may have opened up the possibility for poetry about food in the next class.

In one of her writing assignments, my colleague, Jean Cheney, uses the mapping of space to stimulate memory. On the spot, I decide to do something similar with food. I tell the students about "My Father and the Fig Tree" by Naomi Shihab Nye, the poet I read at orientation, and let them know we will talk about that poem during the next class.[1] Nye's mother is American, her father Palestinian. Her work often reveals a concern for cultural differences and the possibility—and difficulty—of building bridges linking them.

On its most fundamental level, Nye's poem is about longing for a land left behind in the move to a new world. It is about figs and the memory of culture and landscape. Because many of the students in the class are immigrants or refugees, they will have felt a similar sense of loss, fleeing from the familiar to the unfamiliar. This poem will be perfect, I realize. It will invite the class to see themselves in a poem about food.

Nye's poem could be the entrance into other poems about food by Pablo Neruda, Ben Johnson, William Carlos Williams, Stephen Vincent Benet, Elizabeth Bishop, William Wordsworth, Shakespeare, Langston Hughes, Emily Dickinson, and Seamus Heaney.

We are halfway through the evening, and I have yet to discuss the syllabus. I suggest that we take a break. Atiyah's question—a distraction and a gift—has led me to reconsider the whole trajectory of this class and my planning for the second one. I know, now, that when we return to class the following week I will bring the following things: (1) Nye's poem about her father and figs, (2) a journal topic to write about a memory connected to food, and (3) a bowl of figs.

"How'd I do following the syllabus?" I ask my two student teachers during the break. Beth answers, laughing, "Not very well."

"True, but what did we get from following the flow of the conversation? What can we take from the detour?"

"Ahmed got the food bit. He had a pretty good grin when you talked about the bread," Taylor says. "I didn't know you could speak Arabic."

"It might be the only complete sentence in Arabic I know."

"All of them were nodding their heads when you talked about living someplace else and when you talked about food." Beth thinks for a moment and offers an idea: "What about a poem about food?"

"That's a good start." I can feel the teacher coming out in me. For the three of us, I hope this class will become a working lab. "If we teach the students, the subject will come."

Beth and Taylor look uncertain.

Returning from the break, I explain we will read and write poetry during the course, write and respond to essays, and keep a journal. And the class will read two novels. As I talk about the two books I've selected—*To Kill a Mockingbird* and *The House on Mango Street*—I am happily surprised to discover only three students have read either of them.

One of the students mentions that *To Kill a Mockingbird* was written a long time ago, while *The House on Mango Street* is relatively new. It is a perfect moment to discuss that literature is alive, that, as an art, it is constantly evolving because readers see in past depictions of social issues and conflicts those of their own time. To demonstrate, I ask the class to open to the first chapter of *The House on Mango Street*. It is only a page. I read the chapter aloud, then ask the class what it is about. Silence. Pedro offers a thought. He and his wife, Maria, both from Mexico, are taking Venture together.

"The girl is from a very poor family," he says shyly.

"But," another student adds, "she doesn't know this until the nun makes her feel poor."

"Why is that important?" I ask them.

Another voice takes the point deeper. "When the nun points to the building the little girl lives in and says, 'You live there,' the girl is embarrassed."

"Why is that significant?"

Diana responds immediately, "Because nuns take the oath of poverty, and it might mean the nun didn't realize anybody could be that poor. And it's the first time the girl has ever thought she was poor."

By the time we finish discussing the first chapter, I've recorded a list of student comments on the whiteboard that includes poverty, stereotypes, prejudice, the American dream, and loss of innocence. The students recognize all of these as belonging to their lives as well.

It's critical during the first class that I begin to develop and model the idea that art, history, and philosophy can all be accessed through literature. I want the class to think like poets and writers, to climb into the skin of others, to explore the social issues of race, gender, and prejudice through the language of the text. If I can get it right, an assignment that I design for Cisneros's novel will reinforce the poetry we read, allow students to find comparisons with their lives, and create a bridge to our second novel, *To Kill a Mockingbird*.

I ask students to convert the first chapter of *The House on Mango Street* into a poem for the next class meeting. They are clearly confused by the assignment, and I want them to be.

"How do we do that?"

"I don't know. I guess you'll have to figure that out."

"Are we supposed to keep all the words in the poem?"

"That's a good question."

"But are we?"

I ask them what the difference between the text of the first chapter and that of a poem might be.

"Poems are shorter."

I invite them to look at the list on the board and underline the most significant parts of the text in the first chapter. A few students look nervous about underlining in their books.

"These are your books, and you can underline in them," I explain. "In fact, we encourage you to do that in all your books." Pens and pencils begin pressing on the page.

I ask for volunteers to share the lines they've selected and then explain why they're important. As they read, the class begins to see a pattern unfold.

"It's sort of like an outline," Diana notices.

"And we've all got different things underlined."

"It's like the most important stuff we see after rereading, right?"

"Right. And we call this close reading," I reply.

To complete the assignment, the students will have to take the first chapter apart and reconstruct it as a poem. They'll need to decide which are the most important issues for the narrator and then compress this information into a poetic structure. It will be up to them to decide how this looks on the page. Will they create stanza breaks? Will they use the language of the chapter or develop their own? Asking them to create a poem, without talking about the lexicon of poetry, will allow me, during the next class period, to define words like stanza, free verse, alliteration, meter, and end stops by using examples *from their work.*

As we leave the building after the first night in class, Taylor and Beth are clearly excited. Beth speaks first: "I love the students. They are so brave."

Taylor, a tall, bearded poet, thoughtful and reflective, clearly moved by the evening, says, "I felt like such a phony around them. I sometimes think I've had a difficult life, but I haven't at all. I have had a very privileged life. I'm going to learn a lot by being here."

Then Beth: "Wouldn't it be great if all university classes could be like this?"

The first class is important because it offers insights into each student's personality. Who volunteers? Who is uncomfortable speaking but will if called upon? Which students struggle with English and need help understanding assignments?

Of equal value—and perhaps more revealing—is our second class. It will establish the academic tempo and rhythm for the remainder of the semester. I'll see the percentage of work completed, the degree of competency, and begin to get a feel for the common problems students have with comprehension and the mechanics of grammar. If I'm successful in the first two classes, four things will have happened: the class will begin to bond, we'll find common ground among different cultures, we'll begin to unlock the mysteries of literature, and we will laugh together.

At the beginning of our second class, I ask Beth and Taylor to ask the students to take out the poems they've created from chapter 1 of *The House on Mango Street.* From my vantage point at the back of the classroom, I see notebooks open and folders withdrawn from backpacks and hear papers shuffling. Within minutes, almost all the students have a poem sitting on the desks in front of them.

Beth asks for volunteers. Hands fly into the air. The shyness from the first class has disappeared. Students want to weigh in with their work. The poems vary dramatically. Those who weren't certain what to do wrote out the entire chapter but stretched it into a vertical piece of work so that it looks like a poem. Hearing their classmates' work, they are certain they have done the assignment incorrectly. Taylor and Beth assure them there was no right or wrong way to do the assignment. Several other students created minimalistic poems, highlighting and reshaping the words into powerful stanzas. In the discussion, students make serious and thoughtful arguments for the content and shape of their poems.

"Listen, before we turn to Naomi Shihab Nye's poem that I told you about last time, I have a very important assignment for you," I say. "Beginning with our next class, come prepared to share your favorite poem. Be prepared to tell us why you love it. Keep it on you at all times. If—twenty years from now—you come visit me in a rest home, and I have no teeth, and I'm using a walker to get about, I'm going to ask you to pull out that poem and read it to me, and I expect you to have it on you. Period."

Students laugh, but then Pam asks, "What if we don't know any poems? We don't have any books in our house." She asks the question, but she is not alone. Others nod.

"Great question." I point to the poetry section in the library where we hold class. "Come early, copy down a poem from that section over there. Or use the lyrics from a favorite song. It doesn't matter how you find one but be prepared if I call on you."

Then I read Nye's poem:

> For other fruits, my father was indifferent.
> He'd point at the cherry trees and say,
> "See those? I wish they were figs."
> In the evening he sat by my bed
> weaving folktales like vivid little scarves.
> They always involved a fig tree.

The poem is delicious. We discuss nothing about the form or meter. Instead, we talk about our individual connections to it. We talk of the poem's story, of ourselves, of a memory about food, of our relatives, of how cooking is an act of love, of how different food tastes in one's homeland than in a foreign place, and of the importance of breaking bread together.

Usually cautious in her comments, Olga talks about how sweet the figs were that she ate as a little girl in Russia. "Not the same here. The old man misses the figs he had in his garden. I do, too."

Maria speaks of the delicious guavas she grew up eating as a little girl in Mexico, and Carlos tells of the joys of preparing and eating ceviche. Lovingly he describes the process of making the dish with shrimp and white fish marinated in lemon and lime. "When I make this dish, I always think of my mother," he says.

Carlos, who is also a returning student, refers to Pablo Neruda's collection of poems, *Ode to Fruit,* that we read together last year. He volunteers to bring the first poem to share with the class the following week with ceviche and fried potatoes. I promise to bring fresh figs with balsamic vinegar because they are in season and a number of our students have never tried a fresh fig before. Atiyah offers to bring a favorite Middle Eastern family dish.

Clearly, this is a class that wants to share. Our next class would become a banquet of memory, food, and poetry. Poetry would no longer be outside of the classroom. It would be inside all of us. From this class on, and throughout the semester, there would be poetry every class period, and the poems I selected would be tied to something we'd read or talked about.

I have to take advantage of this moment. Quickly, before we leave the library, I write two assignments on the board:

1. Read a third of *The House on Mango Street* and come prepared to talk about your ideas with the class.
2. Create your own poem based on food. Think about what we discussed in Nye's poem.

Immediately hands reach into the air.
"How long should it be?"
"The entire length." And then, "You will know when you are done."
"Can I write a long poem?"
"What is the first rule of writing a poem?"
Silence. Puzzled looks.
"There are NO rules!" I tell them.
"That's a yes?"
"YES!"
"I have a hard time writing in English."

"Write it in your own language. Say what you need to say."

"Will you be reading these?"

"Only if I am asked. When we come back to class, I'd like to hear what you wrote."

We dismiss class and Beth, Taylor, and I head toward the parking lot. Beth is curious about Cisneros's novel. We haven't gone beyond the first page. "So, how are we going to handle the novel?"

"What would you do?" I ask.

They decide we should divide the chapters into three sections and the class into three groups. We'll spend the first half of the next class with our groups highlighting points where their lives intersect with the novel.

"Let's try it," I agree.

"One other thing," Beth says. "We need to start with the novel because you get lost in the poetry."

Our third class begins with two students, Diana and Tonya, volunteering to read their favorite poems. Since I had agreed that we would begin with Cisneros's novel, I look at Taylor and Beth with raised eyebrows.

"We'd love to hear your poems," Taylor says. Beth and Taylor listen and respond to the students' reasons for selecting these works. Then— without so much as a hiccup—they break the class into small groups to discuss Cisneros's novel.

The discussions are highly animated. The students have been reading and enjoying Cisneros's work. With ten minutes left before our break, we bring the class back together and list the most significant intersecting points between the novel and personal experience. The list is impressive and brings home what these students have experienced in their lives: poverty, searching for the American dream, identity, race relations, gender bias, cultural bias, prejudice, loss, racial profiling, stereotypes, freedom, language barriers, family, lost dreams, and always being "the other."

We have continued the movement from literature to social issues and the personal narratives of some of our students. Their lives lived in the text we were reading, and the text now lives in their lives. The class is visibly moved by its members' testimonies.

Returning from the break, Olga surprises all of us by volunteering to read the poem she's written. She stands to read:

Agafia's Secret

Many hands knead dough,
but Agafia's breads
had beauty inside.
All night
while the dough rose
she would dream up
beautiful ideas to fill
the gaps inside the dough.
Herbs gathered by her hands
with sun-kissed meat
onion
cabbage
rice
or fruit combinations
with jam
raisins, apples,
and cinnamon—
the possibilities were endless.
On the outside,
Agafia sang to her creations
after reading the morning news
or reading books
or telling stories,
or she'd make dramatic readings
spoken out loud
to whomever would listen.

The class stands to give her an ovation. Olga explains that her grandmother was never appreciated for her thoughtfulness and kindness, not even by her family.

The poem celebrates Agafia's great culinary skills in the family's rural kitchen in Penza, Russia. As Olga explains, her grandmother made herbed bread that would make the house "come alive like a symphony." When Agafia died of cancer—and only then—did the family members begin to realize, to their shame, how dismissive they had all been of her. "Nobody ever thanked her," Olga confesses. "Nobody."

A terrific teaching opportunity has just presented itself. In my backpack, I happen to have copies of Robert Hayden's poem, *Those Winter Sundays,* prepared for my class at the University of Utah. The poem's narrator is a son who reflects back on his childhood and the shame he feels for dismissing his father's generous acts of warming the house on cold Sunday mornings and "with cracked hands that ached/from labor in the weekday weather made/banked fires blaze."[2] I distribute this poem by a famous African American poet from the 1940s.

As we look at Olga's poem alongside Hayden's, we compare the poetic devices that link them and examine similarities in their themes. The class immediately sees how alike they are and that, taken together, they transcend the barriers often erected by differences in race, nationality, and time.

Following Olga's reading, we have more volunteers than we could have imagined. The last person to offer up a poem is Pam. To be honest, I am surprised when she raises her hand because I've noticed she has a difficult time expressing herself. Even though she has volunteered to read, she admits that she feels uncomfortable and asks if I might read for her. Normally I would decline, but tonight there is such a need for her to be part of the class that I agree.

The poem is about the gift of a wooden rolling pin that she and her sister received from her mother and grandmother at Christmas. As young girls, they had watched as the women rolled out biscuit dough with the rolling pin. "Someday, when you girls are old enough, you will each get one of these," their grandmother had promised. And when the girls did, it was a gift of immeasurable importance. The poem is raw and honest. Recognizing Pam's courage in writing it, the class gives her thunderous applause.

Pedro writes about his mother's cooking. Maria, about the delicious guavas she grew up eating in Mexico. At the end of her poem, we set up our food. I deliver my plate of figs, and Atiyah sets out spicy lamb rolls.

We have about fifteen minutes before class is dismissed, which I use to pass out a copy of Mary Oliver's poem, "The Journey."[3] It is the most important poem we will read during the semester because the themes so obviously and completely parallel the lives of our students. The idea of the journey, in fact, is woven into the entire Venture Course—from its name and the brochure we use to recruit students, to our orientation when we walk up the long ramp to the library's rooftop garden and talk about the journey we are about to embark upon. We have to read this poem before leaving class, and we have to talk about it.

Although in many ways an obvious poem, "The Journey" is a great discovery for students. It provides the first moment when many see themselves in the world of poetry.

Structurally the poem is one long stanza. The device is splendid for the sense of urgency created in the opening lines and sustained until a radical change in voice awakens the reader to the ultimate realization that we are the only ones who can save ourselves.

When, quite accidentally, I used the poem the first year Venture began, two of the students began to cry while I was reading it. When we took a break, I asked them if they were okay. Judy, who would go on to graduate from the University of Utah after Venture and become an adjunct professor in documentary filmmaking, spoke first: "This is a poem about my life. It's a poem about all of us in class. It's a poem about doing what you must do to save your life."

Beth, Taylor, and I leave the class that evening physically and emotionally drained. They express surprise at how hard the students work and how brave they are in writing and discussing their poetry.

"I've only had a couple of classes at the university where students were so comfortable with each other. They felt safe." Taylor is shaking his head. "It was really cool."

"It's important," I reply. "And it always happens with this poem."

"I think next class is going to be big," Beth adds. "I was watching you read the poem to them, and they were totally into it."

"It's because they've lived the life Oliver describes. It's a chorus they know intimately. Their choice to step into the Venture Course is more than an act of bravery. It indicates an awakening that requires action."

When we begin the fourth class—before I can ask for somebody to volunteer to read a favorite poem—two students suggest that we call on Atiyah to read a poem she'd written for one of our journal assignments that came from *The House on Mango Street*. I assume they must have been discussing it with her before class and, for some reason, believe it's important for her to share it. The journal assignment was about personal safety: *Write about a place you feel most free to be yourself.*

Normally Atiyah is a little shy, reluctant to volunteer to read her work, but on this occasion, she doesn't hesitate.

"It's not a poem about my journey. It's about something else. It's about something that happens to me."

"We'd love to hear it," I encourage her.

> *Hijab Freedom*
>
> I see the stares
> aimed at my covered head.
> Terrorist!
> Less than Man: Woman
> Defined, not acculturated.
> My head is covered in God's mantle,
> God's will,
> God's love.
> A warm fabric
> protecting me from
> unwanted desires,
> fashion statements.
> My covering
> unwinds at home.
> The opening of a present
> to grandparents
> grandchildren
> cousins
> uncles
> aunts
> nieces
> nephews
> children and especially
> to my husband,
> my true companion
> in this world
> and at home,
> in this place
> of greatest intimacy
> and trust.

The class erupts in applause. They know what Atiyah wrote about is true. She framed her experience so that almost every student who had felt discrimination and prejudice could relate and feel exonerated. The poem gives them a sense of validation, the feeling that they are not alone. Every student requests a copy. Atiyah has done something that neither Cisneros's book nor I could do: she has given voice and permission to the rest of the class to rise above the weight of judgment and declare their manifesto.

Following the reading, we work through the second third of *The House on Mango Street,* and the conversations get deeper and more reflective. The class understands what the main character, Esperanza, feels as she begins to know that she will have to leave her family and community if she is going to realize her dreams.

That night we don't take a break because the students want to get to their journey poems. Every student has come prepared to read. There is a solemnity in the class we haven't felt before.

The poems are beautiful and heartfelt. There are tears. We have students who become so emotionally involved in their poems that they can't finish. When this happens, another classmate steps up to read on their behalf.

Moments like this are the reason teaching in the Venture Course means so much to me. It is here, at almost precisely the same time every year, that students move from the invisible horizontal world of everyday life into the vertical world of the humanities, of poetry. "The Journey" demands that we consider breaking the bonds and expectations of our previous world and begin exploring a new world to save our lives.

Maria's poem speaks of the love she feels for her son and explains how she has embarked on this journey so she can have a better life and be a role model for him.

Ahmed's journey toward his future includes stepping into the Venture Course. He sees this as the beginning of something wonderful. Similar to the narrator in Oliver's poem, voices in his life were asking him why he wanted to do such a thing. He replied to those voices that he was seeking knowledge. Without education, he would never be able to better himself.

Yolanda speaks of the pressure from her family and shares the underhanded comments and chiding she receives from her husband because she is taking classes that "don't really mean anything."

Pam tells the class that her work schedule has changed so she will not be able to attend Venture any longer. She explains that she can't let that happen. If she has to, she will quit her job. Venture means too much to her. In an aside after class, she asks me to tell the other teachers that if she doesn't return, these classes have meant more to her than anything in her life. Ultimately Pam convinces her employer to allow her to finish the year and graduate. At graduation, she tells me with a big smile, "Those first five sentences of that poem changed my life."

At this moment in the course, the tide has changed, and we can all feel it. The students have found their voices. They are standing upright and declaring their dreams and hopes to each other. They are sending their narratives out into the universe through poetry. They will never withdraw these declarations.

From this moment on, time in class seems to accelerate until we find ourselves at the dress rehearsal for the Winter Celebration, when students share work from the first semester with family and friends. It is the most nerve-wracking part of the first semester. By the time we reach this point, we have bonded deeply as a class and family. Students have gained confidence in themselves and acquired a greater appreciation for the struggles their classmates have overcome. They have grown. But to take their work and read it aloud at the Winter Celebration before an audience that includes not only their families but absolute strangers is a great deal to ask.

Part of what we believe happens in the Venture Course—a transformation that moves toward self-confidence—will occur during Winter Celebration. But before that evening, there will be last-minute jitters, tears, and threats of not showing up to read. In the end, the students will all come, and they will read. When they are done, their families will understand that they are changed people. Their families will recognize something different in them but may not know what it is.

At this moment, neither the students nor their families may be able to pinpoint exactly what the change is, but the Venture faculty knows. That elusive quality is the power of the human spirit to know and assert itself. Through their study in the humanities, students feed the hunger and curiosity we all feel and know themselves in new ways. And the teachers understand that even at our very best, we are simply guides on this remarkable journey.

NOTES

1. Naomi Shihab Nye, "My Father and the Fig Tree," *19 Varieties of Gazelle: Poems of the Middle East,* 6.

2. Robert Hayden, "Those Winter Sundays," in *The Norton Anthology of American Literature,* ed. Judith Tanka, shorter 6th ed. (New York: W. W. Norton & Company, 2003), 2669.

3. Mary Oliver, "The Journey," in Roger Housden, *Ten Poems to Change Your Life* (New York: Harmony Books, 2001), 9.

4

ART HISTORY

From Sight to Insight

HIKMET SIDNEY LOE

Art is not what you see, but what you make others see.

—EDGAR DEGAS

When my four Venture colleagues invited me to join them to teach art history, I was elated. Having admired this program for years, I was excited to embark on a new teaching experience. Then the questions began to bubble up. Could I make art history come alive for these nontraditional adult students? Could I transform our classroom into a meeting space where each student engages with works of art? How could I lead them to understand the place art holds in our lives, in the life of our community, and in human history? I even dreamed that this course would enable Venture students to find universal elements in the diverse art we study from many of the world's cultures. As a veteran art history teacher, I felt a surge of new energy.

As I began to plan course content, a more urgent question arose. Would Venture students find the study of art history relevant to their often-difficult lives? I kept this question in mind as I determined the theme that would drive the selection of course content, works of art, and assignments.

The art history courses I teach at Westminster College come with the gift of time. We can explore an entire era of art during the four hours of class each week and continue for fifteen weeks. With Venture, we are in the classroom just two hours a week for eleven weeks. I was forced to discard much of the content I usually covered. Venture required a new teaching model.

I started with a new text, Carol Strickland's *The Annotated Mona Lisa: A Crash Course in Art History from Prehistoric to Post-Modern*. Strickland's book is heavily illustrated and has accessible, engaging essays explaining artistic periods and styles. She offers many examples comparing and contrasting civilizations, eras, and works of art. This text supports my goal of introducing Venture students to the enormous range of artistic expressions over the course of human history while still showing the continuities that link them.

Venture students bring knowledge of many cultures to our shared classroom, a welcome complexity that is not typical of many college classes and that I make use of during our time together. But, like most college students, they lack the language to talk about art. Before studying the history, then, I introduce concepts and words that they can employ all semester to talk about what they see.

Strickland writes that "there is a world of difference between viewing a work of art and really seeing it—the difference between sight and insight."[1] She understands that to *really* see, one needs language to guide the act of seeing. I follow her choice of French artist Théodore Géricault's *The Raft of the Medusa* to introduce the formal qualities of art: composition, movement, unity and balance, color and light/dark contrast, and mood.

During our first class together, I project the painting on the screen and ask students to write down everything they see. Then they put aside their writing as we discuss each of the painting's formal qualities, one by one. Each slide presents the same image but with a different focus—first on composition, then movement, on down the list. By the time we discuss unity and balance, most students are contributing enthusiastically to the conversation. Suddenly, they have the words and concepts to help them see what they have never noticed before.

Théodore Géricault, *The Raft of the Medusa*, 1818–19. Oil on canvas, 16'1" x 23'6". From the collection of the Louvre in Paris. Photo from Wikimedia Commons.

At the end of this class session, I ask students to describe Gericault's painting. Emily wrote, "I usually try to feel out an art piece by the emotion first, whereas now I can see the dimension of the shading and shapes. The bold horizon and the recurring themes that the artist used."

Suddenly, the painting had meaning for her. She could piece together the way the parts contributed to the whole. When the class began, some students expressed trepidation about studying art, saying they didn't think they were artistic enough to appreciate art or smart enough to understand it. Now—armed with new vocabulary and concepts—art fascinates more, intimidates less.

Students learn that the circle, square, and triangle are the visual building blocks artists use to give structure, balance, and proportion to their art. Learning additional concepts aids them to see: contrapposto, chiaroscuro, tenebrism, proportion, and perspective.

From our first class, I witness students acquiring visual literacy but also something more. They connect to each other through the narratives of the art—when and why it was created, and how key facts about the life of the artist affect the work. Students learn each work has a story that may parallel aspects of their lives or the lives of those around them.

During the first few classes, I also take time to explain words used in the discipline that can be confusing. The need to do this was brought home to me in one of the first Venture classes I taught. I had begun an overview of course content, mentioning that we would study the art of the ancient Greek and Roman civilizations, when a student asked, "If we're going to study 'a brief history of Western art,' what do the Greeks and Romans have to do with it? Where are the cowboys?" I was momentarily stunned. I had never been asked this question before. The experience taught me not to make assumptions about the information and understanding my students bring to class. *Western art* can have multiple meanings.

Unlike many college-level art history classes that are taught by viewing slides and listening to lectures, discussion is key to teaching in the Venture classroom. To allow time for discussion, I show no more than ten images in each class. I follow other principles: no quizzes or exams requiring students to memorize many facts. They don't need to know a lot of names and dates. While I decide course content, student insights generate discussion, sometimes leading us both off topic, which can be fine—occasionally.

Which artists and topics belong in Venture's art history classroom? Although I include a few examples from prehistory, like Stonehenge, I take my cue from Bridget Newell, Venture's philosophy professor, and focus on the ancient Greek civilization early in the course. From there to the end of the course, I include many examples of global art applicable to our contemporary lives, some from the cultures of our many immigrant students.

Selecting fewer than one hundred works to represent the history of art is a subjective endeavor, akin to curating a tightly constructed exhibition. I choose the works for their importance to art history and the discussion they are likely to elicit. For example, a painting such as *The Third of May, 1808* (1814–15) by the Spanish artist Francisco Goya allows students to speak about acts of war they may have witnessed and to empathize with those caught in terrible violence. As Venture student Rudolpho observed, "Goya did not even give the French army faces to further humiliate their cowardly actions. The victims were savagely slaughtered but through Goya's painting were forever immortalized."

Mexican artist Frida Kahlo's poignant self-portrait, *The Two Fridas,* invariably stimulates discussion. The artist's parents were of mixed

Frida Kahlo, *The Two Fridas (Las does Fridas)*, 1939. Oil on canvas, 5'8½" x 5'8½". From the collection of the Museo de Arte Moderno in Mexico City. Copyright by Banco de México Diego Rivera Frida Kahlo Museums Trust, Mexico, and Artists Rights Society (ARS), New York. Photo courtesy of Schalkwijk/Art Resource.

nationality, represented by her two styles of dress. By portraying herself in double, she presents this heritage but also signifies a deeper divide in her life, a Frida who loved her sometimes-husband, Mexican artist Diego Rivera, and another who was heartbroken over their relationship. Themes of internationalism, self-identity, and love gained and lost resonate with each class that views this work. Many students bring their own stories of mixed identities or troubled relationships to our study of Kahlo's art.

Spontaneous conversations sometimes lead the class down an unexpected pathway. After a brief reference to Stonehenge one evening, along with the many discoveries regarding its development and significance, Lee told us that he had watched a program on the History channel narrated by "top scientists" who informed viewers that aliens had created Stonehenge. He told us he had no doubt of the scientists' authority or the truth of their claims. Fortunately I had recently discussed the *Ancient Aliens* series on the History channel with my students at Westminster College to emphasize the importance of fact checking and critical thinking. I knew that the language in the program often confuses the audience because fact and fiction are intertwined, and the speculations lead the viewer to believe that extraterrestrial beings made some monumental art. I wanted to maintain Lee's dignity but also expose the falsehood that had persuaded him.

I explained that, ultimately, art historians care about the factual information attributed to the work. Who made it, how was it created, is there evidence of documentation, and is there knowledge about the work's purpose as intended by the artist or artists? We do not have a written record of the Neolithic civilization that created Stonehenge, I continued, but we do have scientific evidence regarding the people who made the work and its intended use. I tried to make my remarks neutral so it was clear I wasn't criticizing Lee's comment, but since one of the purposes of Venture is to develop students' ability to sift through information widely available through media today—much of it false or distorted—I didn't want to miss the opportunity to let students know how Stonehenge is regarded by the vast majority of those who have studied it.

To develop thinking skills further, we take a field trip to the campus of Westminster College so that each student can use a computer to experience a rich collection of visual images from museums around the world. Museums supplement their collections with information from many sources. We review the Metropolitan Museum of Art's *Heilbrunn Timeline of Art History* for its depth of resources and the Louvre museum's site, in part because it is home to *The Raft of the Medusa,* with which the students have become familiar. Students explore the sites through a guided exercise in critical thinking. They check authority, authorship, and citations to verify content that can be used in their final paper, which requires them to compare two works of art. We talk further about how museums verify the authenticity of art works before spending large sums to buy them.

As the semester continues, students become adept at laying aside their initial responses to a work of art and developing more informed analyses.

Jacob Riis, *Street Arabs in the Area of Mulberry Street*, n.d. From the collection of the Museum of the City of New York. Photo courtesy of the Museum of the City of New York and Art Resource.

One work that challenges them to do that is Marcel Duchamp's sculpture *Fountain* (1917). Venture student Julia's response to Duchamp is typical: "I would have to say, no matter how I actually feel about the piece, Marcel Duchamp's [work] is nearly one hundred years old and seems like it was done ahead of its time. What an act of rebellion! He paved the way for everyone to call their work, their feelings and emotions, their music, even, art."

A work that perennially prompts discussion is Jacob Riis's 1889 photograph, *Street Arabs in the Area of Mulberry Street*. In his words, Riis chose his subjects "to make the poor of his generation visible."[2] He campaigned tirelessly on behalf of the poor and homeless, which prompted changes in both attitudes and laws. This image and Riis's actions resonate with Venture students and reinforce an awareness of how often we have been a society of haves and have-nots.

Riis's caption for this work invites another conversation. "Today we may find the phrase 'street Arabs' derogatory," I observe, "but was it during

Interior view of the dome of Hagia Sophia, 537. Photo: "Istanbul 036" by Steve Evans. Creative commons attribution 2.0 generic license. Photo from Wikimedia Commons.

Riis's time? What might he have wanted to communicate by choosing this title?" Students find the photograph and the question intriguing. What prejudices that inform our language are we unaware of? Or did Riis want to say something about these children that we might have missed had he used a more commonplace title?

Venture students enjoy discovering the diversity and commonality of cultures in the study of Hagia Sophia, constructed in 537 as a Byzantine church in Constantinople (now Istanbul). It remained a church until it was converted to a Muslim mosque in 1453, after Ottoman Turks had occupied the city. Then, after the country became secularized in 1935, this architectural marvel was officially declared a museum. Venture students from different religious traditions find familiar visual motifs within a building where shields expressing the glories of God in Arabic stand next to glimmering mosaics of the Virgin Mary. The architecture and the church's symbols, reflecting its long history of religious conflict and conquest, dominate our discussion during a class focused on religious representations.

Illiana's final essay summarizes the success of these conversations and others during the semester: "The twenty people in this class have viewed many works of art in a crash course over the last few weeks. We all viewed the same pieces and discussed them, and I would not be surprised if we came up with twenty different responses. Even though we have varying interpretations to these works, we all sat together and appreciated each other's reactions."

Each December Venture students and faculty gather for our annual Winter Celebration to end fall semester and lay the groundwork for spring. Students choose a painting or work they have come to appreciate and share their assignments. Eboo, a student from Sudan, speaks five languages and writes essays that reveal his knowledge of art and history before joining Venture. But his presentation about *Mona Lisa* surprised us that night. He had reworked the brief essay he had written for class and read a much more vibrant one for the celebration. His awe and admiration for this painting showed great depth. The power of his words—carefully chosen, although sometimes expressed in fragmented English—seemed to move everyone in the audience.

Studying the history of art makes clear that people have always expressed powerful ideas and emotions through art. Students also gain new powers of observation and language to communicate what they are seeing. Like the other sections of Venture, art history creates a path into a fascinating world students have only vaguely known before. Once on that path, they want to keep going.

In my quest to become a better teacher, I continue to investigate new modes of teaching these students. I wonder, for example, if the works I have selected from the great sweep of art history best serve our students. In the future, I may adopt a strategy that is embodied in Neil MacGregor's *A History of the World in 100 Objects*.[3] Director of the British Museum, Mac-Gregor explains that the museum's selections span human creativity from prehistory to today with just one image representing each culture.

The simplicity of this approach gains power through the multimedia presentation that accompanies the book: a museum exhibition, interactive museum website, and partnership with BBC radio to create programming. As MacGregor describes, "The objects had to cover the whole world, as far as possible equally. They would try to address as many aspects of human experience as proved practicable, and to tell us about whole societies, not just the rich and powerful within them. The objects would therefore necessarily include the humble things of everyday life as well as great works of art."[4] I envision a Venture art history course in the future that focuses on one work per class and offers such a wealth of information to students.

When possible, we plan a gallery or museum visit during class time. Art is best understood when seen in person, there is nothing that can change this fundamental truth. A partnership with a local museum to bring even one work of art to the classroom would make their learning even more tangible.

Although the cost may be prohibitive, I would like to expand art history resources for the class by providing each student with an individual electronic device. It would be loaded with course books, used for writing assignments and language translation during class, help in searching online sites, and assure communication between students and me. Although textbooks are being replaced in many college art history courses by the kind of online content I've described, I strongly believe books remain essential to the Venture art history course. Having a book on their shelf to keep as a reminder of the course reinforces that learning is ongoing for the students. Unfortunately, this may be the only free access to content some students have. Even in 2016, there remains a digital divide, and many Venture students must visit regional public libraries to have access to the Internet.

But there is another reason to question online learning as a way to study art history in Venture. Part of Venture's mission is to bring people into the classroom for real-time dialogue and to share a common experience through the humanities. The art history component of Venture provides that dialogue and shared experience in ways the other sections cannot—through discussion and analysis of visual images. That art history is a component of Venture delights me still.

For some time, I've been convinced that studying art can change our perspective on the past. Now I have the honor of sharing the importance of that history with a wide and wonderful range of students. As Venture student Eduardo wrote in his essay defining art, "Art is one of the truest ways to record history. It shows the human mind, framed throughout time. It gives a physical recording of how society may have felt during different eras." The art history component of Venture has repercussions beyond the classroom as our students develop the confidence to take their knowledge of the history of art and the ability to see the world around them into their futures.

NOTES

1. Carol Strickland, *The Annotated Mona Lisa: A Crash Course in Art History from Prehistoric to Post-Modern,* 2d ed. (Kansas City, MO: Andrews McMeel Publishing, 2007), x.
2. Sam Roberts, "Jacob Riis Photographs Still Revealing New York's Other Half," *New York Times,* October 22, 2015, http://www.nytimes.com/2015/10/23/arts/design/jacob-riis-photographs-still-revealing-new-yorks-other-half.html?_r=0.
3. Neil MacGregor, *A History of the World in 100 Objects* (New York: Viking, 2011), xiii.
4. Ibid.

5

CRITICAL WRITING

With Heart and Mind

JEAN CHENEY

Writing is like driving a car at night. You can only see as far as the headlights, but you make the whole trip that way.

—E. L. DOCTOROW

"I know why I write," says Marcos. "It's to say what I think, my opinions, for the sheer satisfaction of it. I guess you could say it's for my ego." Marcos flashes a grin as he looks around at his classmates for their reaction. He told us at orientation that he is living in a homeless shelter. Young, thin, with sharp features and eager eyes, his hand has been shooting up often during this first class.

To become better writers is part of why students sign up for Venture. In their applications for the course, they often tell us, "I want to learn to write better to be able to tell my story," or, "I have lots of ideas in my head, but I don't know how to get them down." As their teacher, I have similar goals for them. I want them to experience the pride of putting into words thoughts that have long been buried, or the amazement that comes from writing something true they didn't know they knew. I want them to experience the satisfaction and joy that come from making sense of a difficult text by writing about it.

I know from past years of Venture, however, that when our students begin to put their thoughts on paper, their writing will range from intriguing to incoherent. They may speak with confidence and insight in class, but on paper, their ideas are often a muddle. Many have not written an essay in years; some never have. I feel overwhelmed because I know they have much to say and yet are almost crippled by their fear of not saying it "correctly," or by such weak command of writing basics that their thoughts are incomprehensible.

Because Venture attracts immigrants and Salt Lake City has many refugees, about a third of the class speaks English as a second—or even third—language. Some never learned to write well in their native language. Thus, almost all Venture students feel insecure about their writing, even those who have kept journals or, like Juanita, are poets. They're uncertain what is expected of them in this college course. Negative experiences in school, poverty, discrimination due to ethnicity or gender or sexual orientation—all have undermined their confidence. Most don't have Marcos's bravado.

I have many jobs as their teacher: to persuade them that they have plenty of things to say and the words to say them; to help them access—and believe in—their voices; to give them strategies for reading and analyzing a text and models of good writing; to teach them how to ask probing questions about a text, including those created by their classmates; to help them look at the rough ore of their writing for the jewel that is hidden there; to make them understand that all writers have to work at it. Good writing almost never comes easily. Successful writers revise and revise.

But first, students must realize, must feel in their bones, that writing is an important way to spend their time.

"Besides ego, why else do people write?" I ask.

"We can do it for therapy," Diana says quietly. She's a poised, shy young woman from Brazil with serious brown eyes. "It's a way of processing difficult emotions and experiences." Heads turn. Diana colors but doesn't back down. "Sometimes it's the only way you can really understand things that have happened to you."

From the other side of the classroom, Ahmed adds, "It's to provide a path in the darkness." Ahmed's face is intent, his speech formal, continuing the seriousness he showed at Venture orientation. "It informs others of your experience so that there is understanding, instead of misunderstanding, between people of different cultures and backgrounds."

"And you can do that better through writing than talking?"

"Sometimes, yes. You can think about what you want to say, and people can think about what you write."

"Everything gets slowed down?" I ask.

"And there can be true understanding," he continues.

"Empathy?"

"Empathy, yes. Someone can know where you have been, what you have gone through."

"You can also use writing politically," Yolanda interjects from the front of the classroom, near the whiteboard. In her early forties, a native Utahn, she has an open, confident face as if she is used to confrontations and knows she can survive them.

"What do you mean 'politically'?" someone asks.

"Like Orwell says. Here it is: It's 'the desire to push the world in a certain direction.' You can write to push your opinions out there and make people understand where you're coming from."[1]

The students had read three essays for this first night, all entitled "Why I Write", by George Orwell, Joan Didion, and Terry Tempest Williams—an Englishman from the 1920s, a Californian from the 1960s and '70s, and a Utahn searching for new meanings in the early twenty-first century. I wasn't sure the class would relate to these writers; all were privileged and white. Orwell, especially, writes from a world and time foreign to us. Didion claims to use writing to discover what she thinks and to see where her characters lead her. Williams, a Mormon woman who has rejected many of her faith's teachings but not its culture, writes to recognize and celebrate the ambiguities and mysteries of her life.

Tonight it's obvious that the universals in these writings are speaking to these students. You write for ego and to proclaim, to relieve suffering, and to persuade. You write to understand and be understood. You write to light a path in the darkness because there's always darkness. They grasp all of these truths.

"Writing takes courage," says Pedro, a gentle young man and father from Ecuador who is taking the course with his wife. "It takes guts."

"Why do you think that?"

He becomes shy. I try to help out: "What do you risk, being a writer?"

"You have to really put yourself out there, and that takes a lot of guts," says Yolanda, coming to the rescue. "You have to have the courage to be embarrassed or seem stupid."

The essays gave them language to talk about these ideas, but they already understood why writing is important, not in an abstract way, but immediately, viscerally. Writing could do things for them, as well as to them.

The critical writing section of Venture strives to develop the students' ability to understand, analyze, and argue with the ideas they read, both in the essays we explore together and in each other's work. It aims to help students know how to support an argument and detect illogical or weak reasoning. We start with personal essays, then move to writing critically about what we read together. We usually read Sophocles's *Antigone* during the second half of the course because the students easily understand the central conflict in the play. They know well how intimidating it can be to speak truth to power or feel a stronger allegiance to family than to government.

By the end of the year, I hope they are able to identify and create a thesis, to argue a point important to them. I also hope they can use the rhetorical devices Aristotle identified as essential to persuasion: ethos, pathos, and logos. These are new words for most students, but they easily grasp the importance of the ideas they name. They enjoy finding these elements in others' writing and experimenting with them in their own.

That's an impossibly long list of goals. Even with a writing mentor, who comes from the Salt Lake Community Writing Center every week to help students who arrive early for this extra help, there is not enough time. Even though other subjects in Venture provide writing practice, students cannot learn all the principles of writing well in just eleven meetings over two semesters. But I am resigned to this impossibility. I do what I can to move the students in the direction of these goals, knowing we won't get there, not entirely. The Venture critical writing course starts a process. We sow seeds.

Out of the blue, I get an e-mail from a student who graduated many years ago saying, "I don't write as often as I know I should, to get better, but I write a lot more than before, and guess what—I see improvement!" Another one claims, "I get into trouble questioning all the time, but I like it. I know it's important not to accept opinions at face value." Occasionally we see a letter to the editor in the *Salt Lake Tribune* from a Venture graduate and, once, the photo of a Venture graduate, a former gang member, appeared on the front page of the paper. She was at a pro-immigration rally holding up a sign proclaiming, "What Would Jesus Do?"

Although I bring to my teaching the lessons I've learned in many classrooms, in many states, teaching in Venture feels different to me. The students are more diverse—a man from Iraq sits next to a mother from Somalia who sits across from a young woman whose ancestors pioneered here. A twenty-year-old becomes good friends with her fifty-year-old classmate.

But the students' differences are balanced by something they share that is difficult to name: a drive to learn and make meaning of their lives. I have taught nontraditional college students before. Once, during a night course at an air base in Idaho, a middle-aged airman told me he was "rusty but trusty" and stayed true all semester to that sweet description. But even he and his highly motivated classmates didn't have the desire my Venture students do. This education matters so deeply to them.

To begin the process of learning how to write, we don't write—we draw memory maps. "It can be of a bedroom, classroom, neighborhood hangout, your grandmother's kitchen, a refugee tent, the corner store, a friend's front porch. Anywhere you remember keenly from your childhood or from some years ago," I tell them. "Empty your brain as you draw this map. Get everything you remember down on paper. First, draw the outlines, putting in what was physically there. Windows, chairs, a cot, a stove. Then put in every detail you can. Who was there? What colors, smells, sounds do you remember from this place?"

The room becomes suddenly quiet as heads bend over paper, hands drawing intently. After they finish their maps, I ask them to explain them to a classmate. They describe what the lines and squiggles mean and answer questions their classmates may have.

The poet Stephen Dunning at the University of Michigan introduced this exercise to me at a writing camp in Caldwell, Idaho, nearly thirty years ago. He used it as a reliable way to jump-start writing among both inexperienced and experienced writers. I remember the first time I tried it, the fun I had drawing the small bedroom of my youth, a place of refuge from the teasing of my three brothers—the white curtains with their yellow scallops along the edges, the old gray overstuffed chair where I loved to read, and the brown-stained pine headboard with the built-in book-shelf where, in a hidden corner, I scribbled the names of every boy I had kissed or wanted to kiss.

Since then, I've used the exercise scores of times, and it has never failed. Within minutes, students are engrossed, intently drawing lines and pictures on their papers, pens and pencils moving. When they're ready to talk about their creations, the room buzzes. I walk around, eavesdropping. Maria draws the city swimming pool in Mexico where she learned how to swim. Jennifer draws her grandfather's backyard with a swing, telling her classmate that this yard was the one place she felt safe. Kristina maps her dining room in Russia, where she slept every night with her grandmother, and where the smells of cabbage lingered after dinner.

I stop by the table where Rosa is explaining her map to Anna. Her face is tight. She has drawn a map of the place on a street where her brother shot himself in downtown Salt Lake City. The car with rays coming out of it is a police car with the light turning. The lines are the yellow tape of a crime scene. The stick figure in a dress is her mother screaming. I leave them talking in low tones.

When this mapmaking exercise uncovers memories as painful as Rosa's, I ask myself if I should be using it with Venture students. Their memories are often marked by violence and loss, their childhoods any-thing but peaceful. They don't remember white curtains edged with yellow scallops. But the part that comes next—free writing—gives them private time for reflection on their drawing and their past, sometimes for the first time as adults, and that seems very valuable.

For this first writing assignment, I ask them to write fast and freely, emptying their minds of words they associate with their drawings. "Let the words take you wherever the words want to go and do not worry about spelling or grammar," I say.

I urge them to write a lot, to keep writing, even if they feel stalled. We start writing in class, but I urge them to continue at home.

Build on what you've started here and don't judge it. Just write. When you're finished, let this writing sit a day or two and then reread it. You might start the next draft of this writing with the phrase "In this place," then tell us what happened there. Include whatever a reader needs to know to understand and experience what you did. Remember how you described this place to your classmate. Include all of those details.

We talk about the writing process and the myth that writing well is ever easy. In the beginning, I tell them, most writers don't know where they are going. E. L. Doctorow is helpful here: "Writing is like driving a car at night. You can only see as far as the headlights, but you make the whole trip that way."[2] They'll read their drafts in groups during the next class, and make observations and ask questions of each other as writers do. They will hear where their writing works and where it isn't clear. They will get reinforcement and be challenged—gently, I hope.

At the beginning of the second class, Kristina comes in twenty minutes late. She makes a loud noise, dropping her book bag on the table, then fishes out some papers. I flash her a look. She is interrupting a student who is asking an important question. A few minutes later, when the class is breaking into writing groups, she thrusts a three-page essay into my hands. "Here is my assignment," she says. I skim the first paragraph. It is a neatly typed essay in manuscript form. In perfect English.

"But this isn't a draft, Kristina," I tell her. "And it doesn't sound like you." The essay has been written, I suspect, by someone at a local church that welcomes refugees. Being "helpful" means that a church member typed and edited the piece while Kristina "dictated" her story. I spoke with the education director at the church last year, when this happened with other Venture students, asking her please not to let volunteers write these papers. Students don't get the practice they need, I said, and it emphasizes polish when we are trying to teach process.

The director objected, saying that the students didn't know English well enough to write their stories the way they wanted to and that the most important thing was for students to take pride in their work. She pointed out that "every word came from the students themselves."

Our conversation highlights a problem when two organizations with different goals attempt to serve the same people. In Venture, we don't mind if students struggle; we hope they do. We want them to realize, eventually, that they can write far better than they ever thought they could. We don't expect—nor encourage students to expect—perfection.

But we do expect academic integrity. The work they submit must be their own. The church wants to build immigrants' self-esteem and give them a chance to share their stories. It wants to help students take pride in their culture and history. We want them to learn the writing process firsthand and take pride in the improvement they see in their English skills. We don't have the same goals, and the students are caught in the middle.

"I am sorry, Kristina, but you need to write your own draft for this assignment," I say to her. "You had a lot of help with this essay, but to learn English, to learn how to express yourself on paper as well as you do when you speak, you need practice. We don't expect perfection in Venture, but we want you to try, to do your own work. Please bring in a rough draft so that you can share your work and get your classmates' responses."

Although this situation is specific to her, Kristina is not alone in her struggles. Venture students face much more than academic challenges. The losses they have endured, the dislocations, deaths, and violence many have experienced, are constant stressors in their lives. Kristina is a fifty-five-year-old refugee from Azerbaijan who has come to Salt Lake City alone. We learned from her application and interview that she had had several jobs but often fought with her coworkers and never felt respected. She had read Shakespeare and Turgenev in Russian as a teenager, had been in a loving family. But, for reasons she didn't share, she became a refugee.

I understood her desire to get help with her writing and admired her for seeking a solution to a problem she saw. She was proud. She had little practice or instruction writing English and felt overwhelmed by the task, so she accepted the help offered through her church. But the solution she found wasn't going to help her learn, and my refusal to accept her solution added to her stress.

The evening ends with another, more serious problem. After class, Malicia, a young woman from Liberia, asks to speak to me. I remember her from orientation at the city library. That night she said she was excited to be in Venture, but she had trouble controlling her four young daughters— eight months to eight years old—whom she had brought to our meeting. They were naturally bored and loud in their complaints. Finding care for them while she attended the meeting had not been an option.

Malicia tells me that she does not understand the syllabus I have given her, nor the reading assignments. The vocabulary is too hard. Her spoken English is excellent, so I am caught off guard.

"Have you had much experience reading or writing in English?" I ask her.

"Not much."

"Can you read any of the words in this syllabus?"

"Not really."

I realize that someone helped Malicia complete her application to Venture. Fluent in spoken English (and French), she impressed us with her intelligence and verbal ability. That ability, I now understand, is entirely oral.

"Can you read or write in your native language or in French?" I continue.

"No. I've moved around a lot, and girls aren't supposed to get an education in my country."

My heart sinks. Malicia needs basic literacy instruction. Venture does not provide that. It is not an ESL class, either. I counsel her, explaining that she needs a class focusing on learning to read and write in English. I give her the name of a language service for refugees. I watch her face harden as she hears this news: one more rejection, one more disappointment. She is obviously intelligent, but she is also poor, illiterate, and the single mother of four young children in a foreign country. She has just about every card stacked against her. Eventually Venture may work for her but not now. She gives me one more long look, puts her blue book bag over her shoulder, and leaves.

In spite of efforts to screen candidates, we make mistakes, as with Malicia, or take risks, as with Kristina. It is possible to fool an interviewer, especially since we do not ask students to write a short essay during the interview, something we have considered but rejected as intimidating and cumbersome. We may need to revisit that decision. Taking a student with low English skills, like Kristina, will probably work in spite of the challenges the course gives her and she gives us. We hope that she will learn to trust us and herself and write her own work. But turning away a student like Malicia, after accepting her, is heartbreaking.

Sometimes a Venture student will have so much writing talent that my job is simply to get out of the way. We have had a number of these students. I remember meeting Barbra for a writing conference a few weeks after classes began. She wanted "to get better," she said. I welcomed the chance to talk.

Barbra's face always had an eager expression as if she couldn't wait to tell you what she had just read, or what she was thinking. A large woman, she wore loose-fitting cotton print dresses and heavy-soled shoes. In addition to a host of other challenges, she suffered from lupus and might have dressed this way to accommodate the periodic swelling caused by her disease. A couple of times a week, she drove to the hospital at the University of Utah for shots, a treatment that was containing the disease but not curing it. On the day we met, she had just come from the hospital.

"How are you?" I ask.

"Oh, I'm about the same. The pain is worse some days than others. It's okay today."

She sits down and leans over to unpack the little suitcase on wheels that she pulls behind her because she can't carry a satchel or backpack over her arms. They are black and blue from her shots. She puts papers on the table.

Barbra reads aloud as we sit together. It's a personal essay, inspired by the map exercise, about the winter she and her three kids were homeless. She left her home when her brother-in-law tried to run over her son with his car. The dispute had been stupid, she said, but he had all the power—he owned the house and the car. That afternoon she realized her brother-in-law was willing to do anything to prove his dominance, even kill her children. They had grown up in a religious cult with strict teachings about the subordinate place of women. She had no allies in her family, aside from her children. On the day her brother-in-law tried to kill her son, she packed a few bags, took his car, and left. They spent that night in the shelter.

I try to focus on the writing—on the skill of it—rather than the desperate story it is telling. We've been talking about using concrete details in class, how much it helps a reader to see a scene, hear a voice, be persuaded by an idea. But I suspect that Barbra does this naturally. Her essay is full of details. As I read, I have two tracks going in my head. One is noting the skill of the writing, the natural voice, the perfectly chosen detail. The other is wondering how she could be the warm, cheerful, sweet-natured person sitting beside me after living this life.

"This part about being in the shelter, when the woman tells you to watch your socks that you've put beside your bed on the floor. She said that socks can save your life. Did you know what she meant?"

"No. I had to ask the person in the bed next to me. It's because if you put socks beside your shoes, people steal them. You can wear another person's socks, even if you can't fit into their shoes. In the winter, which is when we were there, if you don't have socks on, your feet can get really cold, and they can get wet—feet always sweat in shoes, even in the winter—and you can increase your exposure and get really sick that way. Even pneumonia. So socks are incredibly important. They can save your life. I didn't know that."

After a few days, Barbra left the shelter. The family had to leave during the day anyway, and sleeping there at night made her fearful. She was afraid someone would hurt her children. She decided it was safer to sleep in the old car she had taken from her brother-in-law. During the day, the kids went to school, and she looked for work, although her lupus made most jobs impossible. At night, she cooked something, anything—frozen burritos or whatever cheap food she could find—on the radiator of the car. They bundled themselves in blankets. They lived like this for six weeks until a church helped her find an apartment she could afford. The family subsisted on the $577 she received each month from Social Security because of her disability and the dollars her son brought home from his job at Wendy's.

The "surround of force" that Earl Shorris wrote about included, in Barbra's case, a community following a fundamentalist religion that "disallowed imperfection." She grew up believing that she was undeserving and unlovely in God's sight. The force included her lupus, which disabled her and kept her from working and which made everyday life—raising three children—a monumental effort.

But the forces arrayed against Barbra also included a family history of persecution. She never understood why her family hated her, but they did. Once, when they were living in Alaska on a military base, another family had a new pair of ice skates, in beautiful blue leather, that they couldn't use. They gave them to her family. Barbra was the only one they fit. But, like Cinderella's mean stepsisters, her family decided that she didn't deserve them. She explained that when they went skating on the lake, they played the game "where you hold hands and skate really fast. They put me on the end. I kept falling down, and they thought that was hilarious. And they would say, 'See, you don't deserve the skates. You don't know how to skate. You keep falling down.' Of course I fell down. My heart was breaking, and I was trying so hard to skate."

"I don't want to stop reading this essay," I tell her. "You had me after the first paragraph." It's true. I have only a few suggestions for her. She wants to know how she can improve, what she can do to make her writing stronger. We talk about a few places that can use more development, a few scenes she can expand. Then—feeling a little silly because it seems trivial—I explain that sometimes she uses verbs in the passive voice, that writers may resort to passive voice when they feel uncertain about making a claim or assigning responsibility for an action. Those feelings seep into the grammar of the sentences.

"For example, you write, 'I was hit,' instead of saying who hit you," I explain.

"I guess it's because I am afraid of blaming, pointing the finger. Of course that's what I should do, right?"

"In most situations, yes."

She vows to attack passive verbs.

"You should consider sending this essay to *Catalyst*," I suggest. "That's a monthly magazine that features local writing. They might take it." She looks at me in disbelief. I am saying this to encourage her but also because it's true. Her writing is that good. She is a reader, and that has helped her know how to construct sentences, but she is also a natural storyteller. She understands pace and how to build to a climax.

"You're a fantastic writer," I say. She turns her head to look at me with an expression of wonder, like a tall sunflower rotating to face the sun.

Ken and Nia from the Salt Lake Community College Community Writing Center come to the next class. Nia describes the mentoring process. "We don't change your writing or correct it. We talk about it with you and ask questions," she says. The class votes and decides that she should come on Tuesdays at 4:30.

Ahmed asks, "Can you stay until 6:30? I get off work at 6:00, can be here by 6:10, so that would give us twenty minutes." Nia says, yes, she can stay until 6:30.

The writing center is open six days each week and is free. It's reachable by the light rail system and is located on the plaza next to the city library, where we hold orientation. Sometimes an enterprising student—with a flexible schedule—seeks help there, but more students can get involved when the mentors come to the library at Horizonte, where the Venture class is held.

The writing coaches at the center understand what we're trying to do. They won't rewrite students' papers or aim for perfection. They listen to what the student is trying to say and ask questions, make suggestions. Part of the challenge of Venture is finding the right community partners, ones with missions congruent with ours. Like a good marriage, good partnerships help you reach your dreams, instead of undermining you. You feel in harmony, instead of at each other's throats.

Even with the structure of the memory map exercise, many of the first papers students turn in are sketchy and undeveloped. That creates a common starting point. Venture students, like beginning writers everywhere, aren't aware of how much information readers need to understand what they, as writers, already know. Students like Barbra are an exception. "You are the experts on your subject," I explain. "But you have to share with your readers what you know or—better yet—show them."

"You can think of writing as ladder building," I continue.

"At the bottom of the ladder is a broad, general claim that is easy to make and that we're all fond of making—like..." I wait for a taker.

"We had a good time," someone says.

"Smoking is bad for you." Ahmed looks as if he may know.

The sentence goes on the whiteboard.

"If we start there, as we go up the ladder, we'll want to get more specific, to give evidence so that the reader understands the truth of the statement we started with. We can use facts, statistics. We can give medical information. Or, depending on our audience and the context of this writing, we can tell a story or include an anecdote to show what we mean. What might we say next?"

Around the table, twenty faces stare back at me blankly.

"Okay, I'll try. If this were my sentence and I were writing a personal essay to show the tragic consequences of cigarette smoking, I would write about my father. I would say that he quit his pack-a-day smoking habit in the 1960s when I was in high school. Research had begun linking cigarettes and cancer. One day he gathered my three brothers and me together in our kitchen. 'I will give each of you a quarter every time you see me light up,' he said. We never saw a quarter. Not one. He never smoked again. But he died six years later from lung cancer."

Lights appear in many eyes. Without raising her hand, Vera says, "Now smoking really does seem bad for you."

"Suddenly our skinny idea has flesh and muscle," I say. "We're beginning to make meaning. We're communicating. We can do this through facts or combine facts with story. A bland statement suddenly leads to the loss of a father." A few nod with that look students get when they understand and know they do.

Distinguishing between a topic and a thesis is always hard for Venture students. It takes a long time for the waters to part on this one, and for some writers, they never do. Like a lot of young college students, they confuse a thesis with a moral. They have a hard time understanding that it is a controlling idea, a claim.

I feel playful tonight and decide to use the image of a pond with a fish in it to make this concept less intimidating. The pond is the topic you're talking about. The thesis is the fish you want the reader to pull out of your writing. It's the point you want to make, but it can't really be separated from the pond. It's a hokey analogy, but it seems to connect. Students read from their papers written after the map exercise about an important place they remember and, together, we try to determine the pond and the fish.

Anna reads her essay about a beach in California she loved visiting as a child. It is a piece about innocence and wonder, filled with awareness that they won't last. "Stunt kites fill the sky; they whip and turn to the rhythm of the wind," she reads.

I walk over and offer her the black marker I've been using to write on the whiteboard. "Take it. Anyone who can write a sentence like that should be teaching this class." Anna reddens but smiles. Her classmates clap.

Anna reads the whole essay, and we determine that her pond is the beach and everything she associates with it—kites, wind, sand, sea. Her fish is the freedom she feels there and the futility of trying to carry it away. She fills a jar with beach sand. "My freedom in a jar" she calls it, smiling at the irony.

"Maybe the thesis is that you can't capture and hold freedom," says Julie. "You've got it, or you don't."

Anna looks surprised that someone has understood her.

"Maybe it's that some places allow you to be who you really are, and that is freedom," says Diana.

We sit with these thoughts, letting them settle.

"Maybe freedom is a state of mind, and you can actually have it anywhere," adds Juanita.

The students are listening with their minds and hearts to Anna's piece. They say what they're thinking and feeling without censoring their comments. Their willingness to risk creates a climate for learning that is a teacher's dream.

Why doesn't a similar climate exist in a typical college humanities class? One reason is that Venture students are older with fewer adolescent insecurities. They are less pretentious, unaware or unconcerned with how "smart people" are supposed to sound. Or they simply don't care to adopt false sophistication. I suspect that there is something else going on, too. Because most have not been in educational settings like this before—where ideas are tested and people are respected, and where they feel their minds stretched and growing—they value this experience more. The students who are left after the first six to eight weeks, maybe eighteen or nineteen of the original twenty-five, are here for good. Unless an illness or job change forces their departure, they're dedicated and determined to cross the stage at their graduation in April.

By December, they begin to be aware that what they're experiencing every Tuesday and Thursday night will end. Although April is still months away, the final night will come. One night after class, Juanita approaches me as I'm packing up my books and papers. "It's true that Venture ends in April?" she asks.

I look at her. She knows it's true.

"I don't want it to end," she says.

"Well, fortunately, we have a while until then, many months." My attempt at cheeriness does not distract her.

"Can't it go on? I just don't want it to end."

I study Juanita. She is mysterious to me. Tall and elegant, she has beautiful skin, the color of strong tea, that she often covers with white powder. She has written about her wise and loving Haitian grandmother who raised her until she died when Juanita was seven years old. Her grandmother taught her about gardens, especially tomatoes and beans. She welcomed her home from school and, while Juanita sat at her knee, oiled her hair as she braided it. While she braided, she told Juanita that she was a gift from God and that her life was a gift to God. She must always use it to honor Him.

In her early fifties, Juanita is raising her grandson with her husband, a tall, slender, and quiet white man. Her husband stayed in the background during orientation, joining our group in the circle but staying silent during the introductions.

Juanita has been writing poetry in Jeff's class and lyrical essays in mine. She loves words. When she reads her papers, she goes slowly, taking time to form each word, holding the paper in both hands, as if cradling the face of a beloved child. The course is not introducing the humanities to her; she made their acquaintance long ago. Why does it mean so much to her?

During the afternoon of one class night, a blizzard descends over Salt Lake Valley. Within a couple of hours, visibility is down to a quarter mile, and highways are clogged with snow. At dusk, rush hour reduces vehicles to a crawl. Students begin e-mailing me, asking whether class will be held, but at 6:00 p.m., it's too late to cancel. Students will be on their way by now. Four make it to class, dazed by the drive. Juanita is the last to arrive. A trip that usually takes twenty minutes has taken her ninety. She tries to catch her breath as she sits down at the table, the shoulders of her brown coat wet from melting snow.

The reason why Venture matters so much to students like Juanita may be simple. Talking about important questions with others has power. This is true for all of us, but especially for those who haven't done it before. They have been waiting, without realizing it, for a way to make more sense of their lives. Philosophy, art, literature, history, writing—all feed a human need for understanding and connection. But once that need has been fed, it isn't satisfied; it grows.

"Was Thoreau an anarchist?" We were starting the new year and the second half of the writing class, when we move away from personal writing to analyze other essays, many of them by famous writers. I assigned "On the Duty of Civil Disobedience" for one of the first classes and was worried how the class would respond. About a third had lived under dictatorships. Some had witnessed civil societies falling apart. Many who live in western states harbor hostility to the federal government, especially over land rights. What would they think about this call to follow one's conscience, even if it leads to law breaking? Thoreau's language isn't the easiest to read. Did they follow him?

Marcos is ready. "Yes, I think so. He didn't like government and wanted to go against it when it was wrong."

Sam, a dark-haired man with serious eyes, objects. "I don't think he was an anarchist. He was more focused on a man controlling his life, not the government."

Often quiet in class, Maria offers her appraisal: "I think he's saying that if we follow the government blindly, we are like Muppets because we are not using our conscience." Sitting next to her, her husband,

Pedro, continues the thought, studiously reading aloud from his book: "Let every man make known what kind of government would command his respect."[3]

Marcos adds, "Well, yeah, but Thoreau wouldn't think many of us are very self-reliant. We don't really question the government."

Kate, new to the course this semester, looks uncomfortable. She is a Utah native and, at nineteen, one of the youngest in the class. "I agree with some of what Thoreau says, but not all of it. What if everyone decided which laws to obey and which ones not to? That would be terrible."

"Kate raises a good question. Could Thoreau's message endanger society? If he's not an anarchist, is his message still dangerous?" I ask.

Juanita shakes her head. "This man wasn't a usual law breaker. In fact, he said how he loved the law. He says that civil disobedience is not to oppose or defile the law but to stand up against injustice that was made into law."

Juanita's distinction opens up the impasse.

Diana continues, "Civil disobedience is only just when the law you're breaking is unjust. That's what Thoreau was arguing for: identifying injustice."

"And sometimes you need to stand up for laws that are just but aren't being enforced. That's another kind of injustice," Yolanda adds. "Hearing Jesse Jackson at the U [University of Utah] last week was just amazing for me. I've decided to become a citizen lobbyist. I'm going to get involved in all of these groups. My family thinks I'm going nuts."

Someone asks, "What do you want to lobby for?"

"Enforcement of child support laws. They're on the books, but no one enforces them. My former husband has never paid anything. It isn't fair. It's wrong. This women's group I belong to is going to the Utah State Capitol next week to talk, respectfully, to lawmakers about this issue. You have to have a nice voice, but if you don't have a voice, you are not going to make things change."

"Is this the kind of action Thoreau was advocating?" I ask.

"Not really," says Juanita. "It was more personal for him. He wanted to take a stand, not advocate for what anyone else did. But if everyone really listened to their conscience and followed it, a lot could change. He wrote about that. It's funny, but the part of the essay that I loved the most was the part about him sitting there in jail. They couldn't touch him, even though they put him behind bars. He used it as a chance to meditate on his life and on his town. That was amazing! I liked that part so much I read it to my husband. Now he wants to read Thoreau.

"You might want to write about that in your essay, Juanita. What does it mean to be free according to Thoreau?"

After class, I talk with the site director about the four students who were missing. Anna and Pam live in the same building on a street that is on her way home from Horizonte. She offers to drop by the books they still haven't picked up for the new semester. We don't know why the other two students aren't there. Will they keep coming? We're entering the tough weeks of January and February, when colds and flu are rampant. If students are well, their kids often aren't, and they must stay home with them. If they miss too many classes, they get discouraged and feel out of touch. They stop coming, and we lose them. It's a keen disappointment to lose students at this point in the year. They will have gained from the interactions they have already had, but they won't graduate, and that will seem like one more disappointment in a life full of them.

Minh Le, the custodian at Horizonte, stands in the doorway, waiting for us to finish. Short and muscular, with a shaved head and almost constant smile, Minh is always energetic, even as he cleans up after us when we leave at 8:30 p.m. We're the last class at Horizonte, and he is a little impatient to finish his work so that he can go home. "Sorry, Minh. We're getting out of here," I say, packing up my papers.

Minh sweeps the floor under the tables, briskly moving chairs as he goes. One night, he told me he has been working at the school for twenty-five years. He came to the U.S. as a refugee from Vietnam after the war. He escaped the war in his country on a boat but lost three sisters on the way. They died of starvation. He hopes to retire soon, he says. Tonight I ask him if he's ever taken a college humanities course. "No, I'm too old for that," he says, pushing in a chair.

I think I'll give him a Venture application next week. There's no telling what essays Minh may have locked inside.

NOTES

1. George Orwell, "Why I Write," in *Why I Write* (New York: Penguin Books, 2005), 1–10, 5.

2. E. L. Doctorow, interview by George Plimpton, "The Art of Fiction," no. 94, *Paris Review* 101 (Winter 1986), http://www.theparisreview.org/interviews/2718/the-art-of-fiction-no-94-e-l-doctorow.

3. Henry David Thoreau, "On the Duty of Civil Disobedience," in *Civil Disobedience and Other Essays* (Repr., Toronto: Dover Thrift Editions, 1993), 2.

6

PHILOSOPHY

Thinking for Life

BRIDGET M. NEWELL

Philosophy is to be studied, not for the sake of any definite answers to its questions . . . but rather for the sake of the questions themselves; because these questions enlarge our conception of what is possible, enrich our intellectual imagination, and diminish the dogmatic assurance which closes the mind against speculations.

—BERTRAND RUSSELL, THE PROBLEMS OF PHILOSOPHY

Jean and I sit at a small table near the window at the Coffee Garden in Salt Lake City. It is spring 2004. My mind races as she describes the new Venture Course in the Humanities. How awesome would it be to offer a philosophy course to students who would not otherwise be given the chance to take one? I love that the course will provide access to higher education to people without the means to acquire it. I believe the students will enjoy the course, and I want to be part of it. Although I will provide any assistance I can offer, I really want to teach in Venture. I am thrilled when Jean finally asks. "Yes, absolutely. I would love to!" I say without missing a beat.

As I reflect on my desire to be part of Venture and return each year, I can point to three reasons: I believe in the power and value of engaging with philosophy; I believe in the equal worth and value of all people (and therefore in the value of providing meaningful access to educational opportunities for all); and, honestly, I found Venture to be a fun, worthwhile experience every time.

For me, teaching philosophy is not merely a job or profession; it is part of who I am. I love the possibilities each new group of students brings. And I believe that studying philosophy not only transforms students' understanding of the value of exploring fundamental questions but also transforms their understanding of themselves. "Doing" philosophy brings self-knowledge, self-awareness, and ultimately self-confidence. Although philosophy is often criticized for being overly abstract, too complex, and impractical, engaging in it can help people develop skills essential for living meaningful lives.

One of the problems with philosophy, though, is that most people don't know what it is or why it is worth studying. Unlike literature, history, art, math, and science, philosophy is not usually taught prior to college. Most people's understanding is based on caricatures, stereotypes, or misinformation. Many think philosophy is the "thing" a guru sitting on a mountaintop contemplating the meaning of life is doing. *Philosopher* often conjures up images of a wise old white man in a toga making pithy, indecipherable statements. Just as likely, the word produces an image of a person who asks nonsensical questions and spends his (not usually her) life trying to respond to them, while the rest of us lead more practical, day-to-day lives.

Given these assumptions, most people either don't care about philosophy or don't think it is relevant to them: "It's too far over our heads; it's what the few overly intellectual people do." Philosophers themselves have often perpetuated the idea that philosophy is for only the few, not the masses. Plato's *Republic* indicates that only the wisest people—philosophers—should be rulers in the ideal city. The elitism associated with philosophy has limited and continues to restrict most people's interest. Yet most philosophers believe, as I do, that the philosophical endeavor is in fact a *human* endeavor relevant to all who can reason.

Much of my interest in teaching philosophy lies in the pleasures and possibilities associated with breaking down the barriers to engaging in philosophy, acknowledging and challenging typical assumptions about philosophy, and helping students see that philosophy is relevant to their lives. I want students to know that this abstract, ancient field can help improve their thinking and decision making.

The answers that philosophy provides to fundamental questions—"What is justice?" "Is there a God?" "What is right, and how do I know it?" "Are we free or determined or something in-between?" and "Does life have a purpose?"—are varied and complex, but they are not final. Philosophers invite us into the conversation to explore the way they answer these questions. In accepting this invitation, we consider where, how, and why we align with their thinking or don't. Engaging in philosophy—exploring our most basic assumptions, clarifying concepts, and attempting to answer fundamental questions—helps us consider what our values are and why we have them. It may prompt us to think more clearly about how we want to live our lives, and it sharpens our skills in critical, analytical, and creative thinking. All of this is essential for living well in a complex world.

Although the issues I've outlined are important, my primary interest in teaching philosophy is not to show that it has practical value. Rather, I hope that through studying philosophy, students learn about who they are. On the simplest level, the challenges that philosophy presents help us come closer to recognizing, achieving, and extending our potential. Philosophy is a difficult, yet empowering, endeavor.

Just as participating in sports or strength training or facing other physical challenges helps us understand our physical potential, grappling with difficult questions helps us learn what we are capable of intellectually. We encourage young children and motivate ourselves to engage in physical activities not only because they are fun and good for us but also because we have found that meeting physical challenges builds self-esteem, self-worth, and confidence. The same is true for philosophy. Developing our intellectual abilities positions us to live a different and—I would argue—better life.

Most of these ideas reflect my experiences with philosophy. As an undergraduate, I had no understanding of what philosophy was until I took a class to fill a requirement during the second semester of my junior year. I was pleasantly surprised and "hooked" by the experience. I took another philosophy class the next semester and distinctly remember thinking—while reading Robert Pirsig's *Zen and the Art of Motorcycle Maintenance*—"I cannot believe people think about these things."

As an English major, I enjoyed reading and could comprehend quickly. However, as I got deeper into philosophy, I had a very different experience: Why did it take me so long to read only one paragraph, and why was the paragraph so hard to understand? (Answer: Immanuel Kant.) In spite of the difficulty, I began to realize through philosophy what I believed and why, and I learned that I was capable of much more than I had imagined. I want my students to experience the same or more.

The opportunity to teach another introduction to philosophy was not my primary motivation to join Venture, however. Rather, it was—and continues to be—the students. While I value the opportunity to be a philosophy professor, I have always wrestled with the question, *am I doing enough?*

Much of the work I focus on professionally addresses issues of equity and social justice, and I have often reflected on the distinction between teaching and learning about social justice and actually *doing* something to make a difference in the world. Over time, I have come to believe that teaching and doing are not mutually exclusive; teaching is in fact a way of making valuable contributions to support social justice. But that does not prevent me from wondering about more direct action and considering ways to reach those who do not have the opportunity to attend college in the first place.

After grappling with this concern for years, I found in Venture the opportunity to address this issue. Venture provided me a chance to live my values more completely.[1] Of course I said yes to Jean.

DEVELOPING THE CLASS

In developing the philosophy segment of Venture, I focused on three questions: What is philosophy? What do philosophers do? What is the value of philosophy? These questions, along with the quotation that opens this chapter, begin my syllabus and frame the course. I start each year knowing that, on the last day of class, I will ask some version of "what is the value of philosophy?" While I don't enter each class period with that ultimate goal in mind, the question informs what we do. Throughout the semester, we explore a range of topics and issues and become familiar with the ideas and work of some well-known philosophers as well as contemporary ones who address issues related to race, class, gender, and identity. In all cases, I want students to be able to see philosophy's connection to their lives.

To further this last goal, I usually schedule at least one class to meet on the Westminster College campus to attend a lecture in the Bastian Foundation Diversity Lecture Series and participate in a reception with the speaker prior to the presentation. When philosopher George Yancy spoke on "Whiteness, Racial Embodiment, and the Challenge of Diversity in Higher Education," for example, Venture students read a short essay by Yancy prior to the lecture to gain some understanding of his thought.

For the hour before the talk, Venture students joined Westminster faculty, administrators, and students at a reception in the faculty lounge, where they met Professor Yancy. During the reception, the room buzzed with conversation. I heard Venture students discussing Yancy's ideas or what we had talked about in our last class. They asked Westminster students about the college or shared a laugh. A few approached Yancy to introduce themselves and ask about his work. Others circled from group to group, as if receptions with a visiting philosopher on a college campus were a daily event for them.

Students engaged in various ways with the lecture itself—some participated in the question-and-answer session, others stayed after the talk to raise questions with the speaker—one-on-one—while he was still in the auditorium, and still others discussed the presentation with classmates in the foyer outside the auditorium.

Experiences like this are extremely valuable to all students. Although many events on college campuses are free and open to the public, before the George Yancy lecture, Venture students may not have been inclined to go, even if the event interested them. Being included among those who are "welcome to attend" a public event is different than being specifically invited and *feeling* included. Having experiences like the one with George Yancy can motivate students to attend other events after the course has ended. In terms of the philosophy course itself, actually meeting the philosopher they just read—seeing a real human being—helps dispel many of their assumptions about philosophy and those who practice it.

THE CLASS

The philosophy section is offered in the second semester. On the first day, entering the classroom is like walking into a buzzing, happy reunion. Students are excited to see each other after the semester break. Although the first semester may have been a challenge, they have had enough time off to realize that they miss that challenge and the intellectual engagement Venture offers. They are eager to begin new subjects and get back to work.

What often surprises me, though, is how welcoming they are to me:

"Hello, Bridget! I have been looking forward to this class."

"What is philosophy? I've been asking myself that, and I really don't know."

"What are we going to do? Do we get our books today?"

We are not strangers, of course, because we have talked at orientation, and I've made an effort to speak to each student at the Winter Celebration that marks the end of the first semester. I want them to know that I am looking forward to our class. But, on the first day of class, I am surprised by their level of interest and enthusiasm.

For all of us, starting the class with a high level of positive energy goes a long way toward easing the transition to philosophy and philosophical thinking. I am always grateful to first-semester teachers for building such a strong foundation and community among the students. Because of their work, I am able to begin the second semester with engaged, eager students who are ready to learn.

Our first semester faculty meetings at the coffee shop have made me aware of some of the difficulties (both personal and course related) the students face, but the students I see are in no way victims of those difficulties, people who have given up or are disengaged. They are resilient survivors. They have the "grit" that is so much discussed in literature about underrepresented populations in higher education. While first-semester courses and professors have bolstered students' confidence and helped them develop skills necessary for successful learning, I believe that Venture students come to us with the characteristics necessary for success. Their hunger for knowledge that brought them to Venture shines through from the beginning of my semester with them and helps shape classroom dynamics.

On the first day of philosophy class, we delve into a lively exchange about philosophy: What is it? What do philosophers do? How and why do they do it?

We start on common ground by discussing stereotypes and other assumptions about philosophy. Part of the point is to let students know that yes, we may share a similar mental picture of philosophers—a man in a toga, sitting on a mountaintop, thinking. Recognizing that we may have these stereotypes, but often little experience with philosophy, allows us to understand why philosophy is an elusive subject for most people. We haven't had the chance to study philosophy in elementary, middle, or high school. Learning anything new can be uncomfortable.

We work together to establish a big-picture understanding of philosophy using the familiar format of filling in the blanks: "Philosophers love to _____ with _____ about _____ for the purpose of _____." Together we supply many words or phrases for each blank. Students call out answers, and I fill in or ask clarifying questions until we have several possibilities in each blank.[2]

"Philosophers love to talk, think, contemplate, ask questions! with other philosophers, anyone about life, why people do what they do, meaning, God, religion, motivations for the purpose of learning, teaching, not sure."

After we have filled in all the options we can, we narrow the focus, and—through discussion—I select those that are best for framing our course. Although I steer the discussion slightly at the end, what is left are usually answers that came from the group. A typical sentence from this exercise reads, "Philosophers love to argue with other philosophers (or anyone who will listen) about fundamental assumptions or questions for the purpose of gaining wisdom."

This exercise allows us to examine the difference between argument and assertion or opinion, and between arguments and verbal fights. We also explore examples of fundamental questions and discuss why anyone (everyone?) wants to gain wisdom. After this discussion and a brief overview of the topics we will address during the semester, we are ready for course work: to read and discuss primary texts in philosophy. Dealing with primary sources is difficult, but we do it to build students' confidence. They know they are not reading a watered-down summary of philosophers' ideas. I use a sourcebook of primary texts that includes diverse voices of philosophers: *Voices of Wisdom: A Multicultural Philosophy Reader.*

I share my experiences from college when I was new to philosophy to let them know that reading philosophy is challenging, humbling, and time consuming, but it is something that we can learn to do. Exploring primary sources also provides the opportunity to examine the nuances of philosophical arguments, not just the main points or conclusions.

I have adjusted the readings each semester I have taught Venture, but I always include Socrates. We read the "Crito," the "Apology," and the "Allegory of the Cave," discussing the latter on the last day of class. Starting and ending with Socrates allow us to reflect on what we have learned from the beginning to the end.

We begin with Socrates for several reasons. Most students, regardless of their background, have heard of Socrates and Plato, so we start with an entry point that meshes with their existing knowledge. In addition, the experience of reading and discussing Socrates's ideas begins to build cultural knowledge that has value beyond the course.

From the second day of class, then, students have evidence that they can engage in philosophical thinking with philosophers—after all, they are doing it. This is not to say that they don't find Socrates confusing or frustrating. Like most introductory students, they have difficulty following the nuances of some of the arguments in the "Apology," but they understand the issues and enthusiastically enter the conversation. They enjoy asking and answering many questions the text raises: Was Socrates really a corrupter of youth? Why was he found guilty? Was he a pest that was actually valuable to society? Should he escape from jail? What were his obligations to his children? Was living in accordance with his principles the right thing to do? Is an unexamined life really not worth living?

Sometimes, months later, an argument raised by Socrates strikes a student as relevant to his or her life. One evening toward the end of the semester, I entered the classroom early to find Lorena, a quiet student, sitting in her usual spot. As we began to talk, she told me that she had been thinking about the "Apology." "Oh, really? In what way?" I asked. She said a friend whom she had looked up to for many years had just committed suicide. In addition to being grief stricken, Lorena said she began to think about Socrates's assertion that an unexamined life is not worth living. Now that her friend—someone she saw as strong and confident, as a mentor of sorts—had committed suicide, she said she was asking herself, "What will I do now? Who will I be?" And in those moments, she said she began to understand, *really understand,* what Socrates meant. She would have to experience and live her own life. She would determine her values and decide for herself where her life would go.

As more students began to enter the classroom, she ended the conversation, but as we exchanged our final remarks, I was struck by the impact that Socrates had had in helping Lorena begin sorting her thoughts and feelings about her future after a friend's death.

After a few classes on Socrates, and to build on a theme raised in the "Crito"—citizens' obligations to adhere to their society's laws—we turn to Martin Luther King Jr.'s "Letter from Birmingham Jail." Focusing on King allows us to bridge thematically from ancient Greece to the 1960s in the United States and illustrates the timelessness of philosophical questions.

Students recognize and enjoy King's reference to Socrates. They know what King means because they have just read this famous philosopher. When discussing the depth and content of King's arguments, students often use the word "profound." They are awed by his arguments. Some remember the civil rights movement, but others have only heard of King. Reading and discussing "Letter" provides the opportunity to examine King's actual words, insights, and arguments.

As they did with Socrates, when they discuss King's letter, students engage in an ongoing historical conversation with someone they recognize or know something about but have not had the opportunity to study in depth. As we discuss the value of developing a good argument, students compare King's style of argument to that of Socrates. They discuss his voice, the feeling they get when reading his words, the power of repetition, and so forth, concepts they learned in the critical writing course.

One year, discussion of King prompted passionate questions about why more people don't have the opportunity to study philosophy. "Why *don't* people have a chance to learn philosophy in high school or earlier?" the students asked. As they spoke, I wished I had a tape recorder. If I had not been in the room, I might not have believed the passion underlying the questions and assertions: "People need this stuff." "Why don't people get to take philosophy if they don't go to college?" "Really, people need this."

In addition, King's letter provides an opportunity for students to evaluate their ideas on equality, racism, and justice with a diverse group of adults. Many students have not had the opportunity for such discussions with people of various racial and ethnic identities before Venture, and they come to see it as invaluable.

Going beyond stating an opinion about an issue to developing careful reasoning about it engages students' minds in a (presumably) new way. It forces them to push beyond the easy answers or platitudes we all receive through the media and, sadly, through some of our schooling. This difficult, but engaging, "pushing toward" an answer that is not already evident is hard and invigorating. Stretching their critical and analytical thinking skills to address fundamental assumptions that matter about law, justice, race, and human dignity puts students in touch with aspects of themselves that they may not have had a chance to nurture.

Despite students' strong engagement with Socrates and King, I know that philosophy class is not always enjoyable. Philosophical thinking and writing are challenging. While this is true for almost all students, the challenge for Venture students feels particularly troublesome to me. At times I feel as if the philosophy course places a hurdle in front of runners who have just established—or are on the brink of establishing—a good pace. Right after they have adjusted their lives to the rigors of the Venture Course during the first semester, they must learn to read and respond to the complexities of philosophy. Perhaps they've started to develop a highly descriptive or narrative writing style for literature and art history, or they have begun to feel comfortable sharing their personal responses to readings. Rather than building on those skills, I'm asking them to shift toward a more critical, analytical writing style and, I assume, more complicated reading assignments. This shift is supported by the assignments in the second semester of the critical writing class, but those are concurrent assignments, not ones they have completed.

To help students cope with the complexity of philosophy, I ask them to think of a hobby or sport they enjoy. What was it like when you started out? Were you immediately good at it? How did you improve? When did you begin to enjoy it? We discuss a typical pattern: motivation to try, initial frustrations with the actual challenge, motivation to do better, pleasure in becoming better.[3]

One goal of this discussion is to invite students to view the hurdles and challenges as signs of learning, not roadblocks. We get better at anything through practice. I hope to provide students with a growth mindset that can be helpful when they encounter other challenging readings and assignments in the future.

This conversation had a dramatic impact on one student's relationship with philosophy and the book we were reading. After we talked about "reading with a pen" to engage directly with the philosophers by asking questions or noting confusing passages in the margin, Dina announced, "I finally did it! I wrote in my book just like you said. I have all kinds of questions to ask about this. I did not want to mark the book because it was new, but once I got over it, I felt fine."

She used her questions to help guide parts of our class discussion. Recognizing that everything won't be clear on the first—or even second or third readings—and that writing in the book reveals engagement with the ideas, not destruction of property, helped us stick with the reading and discussion when the texts were difficult.

Descartes's *Meditations* are especially challenging to students. I often include the first two meditations in the course syllabus. They are short, and they introduce students to significant philosophical questions: Can we know anything for certain? And if so, how? Does knowledge come from sense perception, reason, experience? What is knowledge?

On one level, the discussion about Descartes focuses on understanding why philosophers ask these sorts of questions. On another level, I've selected these readings from Descartes because some may have heard the phrase, "I think; therefore, I am." Reading Descartes provides context for that statement. For those who haven't heard it before, I tell them that, like Socrates's "an unexamined life is not worth living," the statement, "I think; therefore, I am" is a well-known phrase, so this study of Descartes, I say jokingly, will prepare them for any cocktail party conversation about philosophy. We have a little fun envisioning and mocking that scenario and we sometimes discuss why the joke they may hear one day—"I drink; therefore, I am"—doesn't make sense from Descartes's point of view.

More seriously, they know that they can now join a conversation about these statements from Descartes or Socrates, wherever they may encounter them. Whether this actually happens or not is irrelevant. They have done it in class; they have evidence of their intellectual ability to engage with some of the world's greatest thinkers. This, I believe, contributes to strengthening self-confidence.

Descartes's question—"How do I know I'm not dreaming?"—seems absurd to many people. Together we discuss what prompts such questions and how philosophers attempt to answer them. I invite students to draw their own conclusions about Descartes's thinking—and they do.

"What a waste!" a frustrated student once exclaimed in response to Descartes. While this assertion appalled several other students and may have seemed disrespectful to some,[4] it led to an examination of Descartes's motivation for asking such a question. Some wondered if philosophy is a study for only the elite. Who has the time or luxury to sit around and ask such questions? I remind students that it is fine to find some philosophical questions and approaches more valuable than others. Our goal is to understand what the philosophers are doing and why, not necessarily to agree with each argument.

As the semester continues, we may explore patriarchy and the gender of God, feminism (Mary Daly) and racism (bell hooks, George Yancy), the relationship between language and identity (Gloria Anzaldúa), the concept of forgiveness (do we have a moral obligation to forgive?), and the notion of the good life. Although this collection of readings may seem random, it is not. My goal is to illustrate the relevance and value of philosophical thought and have students engage with issues contemporary philosophers address.

Sometimes students reveal their responses to the readings in private comments during a break. "I felt blasphemous even reading this," one woman in her mid-thirties said after reading Mary Daly. "I did not want my sister to see what I was reading." Most of the time, however, students are comfortable making their responses part of our classroom conversation. Students are more or less aligned in their responses to some readings, while others lead to healthy debate. As the course progresses, we begin to explore topics they may not expect to address. In terms of content, I want to introduce students to the range of conversations they can have with philosophers.

Writing assignments are a challenge students and I face, although for different reasons. Initially I was interested in helping students learn to write five-page summary and response papers that addressed key arguments in the texts. I anticipated that students would learn to write a short argument that directly responded to a philosopher's position. More often than I would have liked, however, I received papers that were reactions to the arguments or papers that related the arguments to the student's personal life. Students had little experience in writing essays, other than in the critical writing class, and were nervous about the prospect of completing five pages of writing on philosophy.

I had to make a decision about the extent to which writing this specific kind of paper mattered. So, after the first year, I reframed my approach to writing assignments. I came to see more clearly that the philosophy section is part of a humanities class, not a stand-alone introduction to philosophy. This perspective enabled me to adjust my focus to writing that engages with the issues, not the development or evaluation of a philosophical argument. To be honest, at times I remained concerned about centering on engagement and reflection, particularly when a few students indicated that they wanted to study philosophy in college. Was I setting them up for failure?

This is a shared concern of Venture faculty members: no one section goes into a specific subject in depth. Ultimately, recognizing that our primary goal is to engage students with the humanities, rather than provide an introduction to the specific requirements of our disciplines, helped me significantly as I developed and reviewed writing assignments.

An advantage of teaching the philosophy section of Venture during the second semester is that students are also taking the second half of critical writing and the entire American history course. Jack, Jean, and I do not coordinate the class content, but there are definite overlaps—our focus on writing and topics that we all cover, such as justice, equality, race, and gender. When supporting their claims in philosophy class discussions, students remind each other of topics raised in history. When writing papers, students put into practice the process and strategies learned in critical writing, and, as I've already mentioned, they comment on philosophers' writing styles. Through the overlapping courses, students develop a toolkit to use across subjects.

In terms of day-to-day activities in class, I strive to mix it up and address various learning styles. But I also fall back on some tried and true methods. From the first year of teaching Venture, I have used a storyteller approach that intersperses questions. I see my role as focused on clarifying the content and setting the stage for discussion. Students know that their responsibility is to *read* the whole text but not necessarily *understand* all of it. We work on understanding and responding together.

I usually begin our discussions by checking in with students on the reading to gauge the level of difficulty and their initial responses: How was it? What did you think? What we do that night depends, in part, on the level of understanding and interest they report. If they feel ready at the beginning, we move quickly into discussion of the philosopher's arguments and their reasoned responses to it.

Sometimes the whole class engages in a question-and-answer discussion; at other times, students talk about the readings in pairs or small groups, prompted by guiding questions. Full-group and small-group discussions provide opportunities for close reading and exploration of the text. Taking time to unpack the meaning and encouraging their responses to specific passages and arguments help them focus on building their reading and speaking skills.

ASSESSMENT

Those of us who teach Venture often find ourselves discussing students' responses to the course and the changes we see in them from the beginning to the end. It is difficult for me to map a before and after picture of Venture students. They come eager and ready to learn. I see them enjoying, disliking, and struggling with philosophy. Collectively and individually, they get tired and reenergized and keep trying. A few back out. But most begin with confidence, struggle in the middle, and then leave with renewed confidence. The slight, but important, difference between the beginning and the end is that when they leave, they are aware of their confidence, even if it is limited, and they are clearer about what studying philosophy can do for them and others.

On the last day of class, we watch a video that focuses on the "Allegory of the Cave" and includes philosophers discussing the value of philosophy. After we talk about the "Allegory of the Cave," I ask some version of the question, "What will you take away from this philosophy class?" Here is a list of answers students have offered in their words, as much as possible, including the way they clarified their comments in response to a "What do you mean?" prompt from me:

- "The ability to reason."
- "Inner peace—I've learned that it's okay to question."
- "Skills in articulating ideas clearly."
- "Critical thinking."
- "Conflict resolution—as a result of thinking from different perspectives, I'll be able to resolve conflicts."
- "The ability to identify consequences of beliefs and assumptions."
- "Compassion—we can be more compassionate because philosophy asks us to understand other people's perspectives."
- "Recognizing the difference between disagreeing with a person and disagreeing with the person's ideas."
- "Learning from people who die for the truth."
- "Problem solving."
- "Attention to detail."
- "Patience—take in ideas and think before responding."

While some responses, such as critical thinking and the ability to reason, are predictable,[5] I was struck by others: compassion, patience, conflict resolution, inner peace. Students not only identified particular *skills* they would take from the course but also character *traits* that could influence their interactions with other people. Their insights were unexpected and powerful, especially compassion. I had never considered that philosophy taught compassion, but I now saw how it can and does.

Our conversation about the value of philosophy prompted one student to assert that one class discussion left her feeling as if she had been "slapped in the face by a strong dose of wisdom."[6] I thought of the sting of a gadfly and let her know that Socrates would very likely appreciate her description. Returning to Socrates's analogy of the gadfly allowed us to come full circle—starting and ending our class with a discussion of his "Apology."

Philosophy is hard. It may not become the favorite class of most Venture students, but they leave the class knowing what philosophy is and what philosophers do, and they are able to discuss and debate its value. More importantly, they know that they have participated in difficult, complex conversations. They know themselves slightly differently—not only in terms of what they hoped to do—as was the case when they began the class—but what they have done and are capable of doing.

NOTES

1. As a white, able-bodied, straight, middle-class woman, I have studied issues of privilege, power, and resistance. I have also lived a life that has made obvious to me that paying attention and engaging in meaningful ways with individuals and groups whose backgrounds and experiences are different from mine has helped me develop a more informed critical lens for understanding the world. Given all of this, I knew Venture would be a two-way teaching and learning experience. This critical lens also helped me recognize and respond to implicit (negative, deficit-based) assumptions that entered conversations about Venture or Venture students. However, I know my privileged position also impacts what I do *not* see or notice. Recognizing this, I remain focused on doing my best to keep my lens broad, deep, and sharp for our students' sake.

2. Kessler, *Voices of Wisdom*, 2–6.

3. I'm sure I did not invent the concept in this conversation. Participation in a National Learning Communities Conference at The Evergreen State College in Olympia, Washington, in 2004 introduced me to this line of thinking.

4. One student apologized for the other student's "disrespect" toward me after class. I assured this student that questioning the value of a philosophical argument is doing philosophy and that disrespect was not what I felt.

5. These predictable comments may have been "primed" through the video.
6. I referred to this quote in another book chapter: Bridget M. Newell, "Being a White Problem and Feeling It," in *White Self-Criticality beyond Anti-Racism: How Does It Feel to Be a White Problem?*, ed. George Yancy (Lanham, MD: Lexington Books, 2014), 134.

AMERICAN HISTORY

Preparing Voices for Democracy

L. JACKSON NEWELL

For here we are not afraid to follow truth wherever it may lead, nor tolerate any error, so long as reason is left free to combat it.

—THOMAS JEFFERSON

Tom is about forty, angular and slightly rumpled. He speaks deliberately to his peers in my American history class. "For this week's assignment, we were supposed to interview and write about the memories of two people who lived through World War II. Between my work as a bartender and school, however, I had no time to do this. But," he continues, "two old veterans come into the bar every afternoon about 4:00 to nurse a couple of beers and kill a few hours. Turns out they both fought in the South Pacific, so for a couple of days I pumped them for their war stories. The longer we talked, the more they opened up."

He turns toward me: "These conversations weren't technically interviews, but I went ahead and wrote down what I learned from them anyway." He reads from wrinkled papers in his hands. His words bring distant events to life as well as the intensity of his subjects' long-dormant feelings. He pauses, then reflects briefly on the irony that these men could remember painful, even deathly, events with such savor. Twenty-three classmates brighten with spontaneous words of admiration and a barrage of questions. "Did they suffer from PTSD [post-traumatic stress disorder]?" "Do they still hold a grudge against the Japanese?" Unaccustomed to such attention, Tom blushes, and a little grin creeps across his face.

The raw potential for teaching American history to Venture students has shown through. Drawing on a wealth of dangerous and difficult life experiences, Tom improvised easily. He wrote with refreshing directness, using verbs that crackle. As he recounted these war stories, no one in the room looked to me for a reaction as undergraduates often do; rather, they seemed to trust their thoughts and feelings and voice them.

Here students do not assume that authority or position renders sound judgments. That is a privilege Venture professors must earn. When the students eventually do look respectfully toward me for my critique, I share a few observations, express my admiration, and then prod the students to continue. Others take their turns reporting work on their interviews with new confidence in their powers of observation and their distinctive styles. This is American history, Venture style.

In this course, I want to engage students with our nation's past. I hope to inspire them with a sense of urgency to raise their increasingly informed voices to shape its future.

We start the semester with a close look at pre-Columbian America, followed by an examination of early contacts with European adventurers, conquerors, and missionaries, and then trace the economics and politics of British, French, and Spanish colonialism to the American Revolution. From the Declaration of Independence to the Constitutional Convention of 1787, we come to see the revolution as unfinished work. No political movement in history was justified by loftier ideals or energized by more universal principles, but the self-interests of its leaders and the ironies of practical politics left many dreams of liberty and justice stillborn.

Those dreams still haunt and inspire us, and each new generation of Americans must supply and support its own "trustees" of our noble ideals. "Under our watch, in your time," I challenge my students, "will the revolution progress toward its ultimate realization, or will you and I let hard-won advances in human rights and democratic institutions slip sadly away?"

Angelina responds instantly: "Until now, I didn't have a clue how grand the founding ideals were, or how awful our record has been in living up to many of them. But I feel driven to make America's experiment in democracy work. God help us if we fail." Her sentiment draws approving nods from around the room. Then Jessica asks with earnest intent, "Yeah, but what can we do, seriously?" Inspired by her prompt, we are off to a well-grounded discussion.

The American Revolution has become a living presence in our class, not a distant war or a series of important old documents. And the onus is on us now. Instilling this sense of responsibility and urgency is my passion. I know I cannot succeed without confronting my students with some terrible realities as well as many honorable achievements in our nation's past.

I began teaching this way in Venture with trepidation, wondering how refugees, undocumented immigrants, and homeless citizens would respond to Jefferson's slaveholding, the tragedy of Wounded Knee, Ku Klux Klan lynchings, or the My Lai Massacre. I should not have worried. Because they knew about these ugly incidents in our past, the words and actions of Martin Luther King Jr., Susan B. Anthony, Crazy Horse, and the civil rights or antiwar demonstrators of the 1960s only stirred my students to study harder and with greater purpose. I had underestimated their appreciation for unvarnished history and their pride in a country that has struggled persistently, if sporadically, within itself to right its faults and reverse its failures. To my surprise and satisfaction, students began attending PTA meetings and joining protests for fair housing. One started a "walking school bus" project so that parents could take turns shepherding their children to school safely.

TAKING CHANCES

How did I come to see teaching as preparation for democracy? With a penchant for adventure, as far back as high school, I rebelled against the passivity of formal education. I enrolled at radically innovative Deep Springs College, where students participate in every facet of the institution's governance, including hiring faculty, and accept responsibility for providing labor and some management direction for the associated farm and ranch.[1] I graduated from Deep Springs, determined to apply the philosophy and practices I had experienced wherever my educational path took me.

As a result, mine has been an "edgy" career. Repeatedly I have been lured out of the mainstream of college teaching into the turbulent cascades and tributaries of experimentation. Striving to advance the spirit of liberal education as a professor at the University of Utah and, later, to challenge gifted undergraduates at Deep Springs College, I read Earl Shorris's article about his Clemente Course in *Harper's* magazine in 1997. I resolved then to try something similar in Utah when I finished my service to the students at Deep Springs.

That chance did not come immediately, but when I retired as president of Deep Springs in 2004, it happened fast. Upon returning to Salt Lake City, I found myself on the ground floor of planning the Venture Course with four colleagues. My experience primed me to accept the challenges that Venture offered, to encourage adults who struggle (for any number of reasons) to start over. I wanted them to understand the potential of historical knowledge to help them gain control of their lives and participate in shaping our common future.

I was immediately engaged by the budding educational philosophy of Venture and the challenge of applying it to teaching American history. Fruitful conversations with my faculty colleagues has shaped my teaching in Venture, but I have also been enriched by my chosen field of study—the history and philosophy of higher education with an emphasis on teaching and learning in progressive colleges and experimental undergraduate programs.

It seemed to me that a similar gamble outside my comfort zone was appropriate. When the five of us came together early in 2005 to plan the Venture curriculum, I was not the obvious pick to teach the history segment. I had been teaching social-justice and leadership-philosophy courses for honors-level scholars and graduate students for many years. But I had earned my master's degree four decades earlier in eighteenth-century American and European history, taught in that arena for six years, and then returned for a doctorate in the history and philosophy of universities. What if I took a chance, too, and bargained to teach in an area I had not touched since early in my career? In choosing to do this, I was emboldened by Paulo Freire's apt observation that "whoever teaches learns in the act of teaching, and whoever learns teaches in the act of learning."[2] Thus began my reeducation.

A WILD ORGANIZATION

Starting with the nature of our organization and the composition of our faculty group, our Venture project was a rare example of the benefits and limits of a *wild organization*—one that germinates or grows largely outside established institutions. In an era of increasing institutional size and bureaucratic standardization in education, government, business, and journalism, we have lost much of life's spontaneity, creativity, and even joy. Part of the genius of Utah's Venture Course is that it sprang up and grew largely outside stifling bureaucratic boundaries. Giving us unusual latitude, Westminster College trusted us to set the standards for our curriculum to qualify our students for eight semester hours of humanities credit.

Another key factor in creating our Venture humanities course was that each of us had volunteered to join the enterprise. None of us was assigned to the team. There would be modest paychecks, nicely reinforcing the esprit we felt in creating and teaching our Venture curriculum, but the money was not generous enough (about $3,500 a semester) to be a primary motivator.

From the beginning, we held our faculty meetings around a corner table at the Salt Lake Roasting Company. We fell naturally into a Quaker-style consensus ethic to shape every aspect of developing our curriculum, pedagogy, and program culture. These conditions produced a heightened sense of responsibility to each other and our students, released imaginative energy, and created bonds among us much faster and far tighter than any of us had experienced with our university colleagues. What we have built together in Venture owes much to the unusual nature of our enterprise.

With no dean to satisfy and no curriculum committee to second-guess us, our sense of ownership generated new energy and ideas about teaching. Classroom cultures often mimic the spirit and morale of the college or university where they exist. Over time, our students' growth increasingly reflected our development as teachers. Our classrooms became microcosms of the free and responsible dynamism that produced the Venture program itself.

In the best sense, our Venture classes were as wild as our little organization. Discussions typically echoed the same high levels of freedom, energy, and responsibility that we reaped as faculty in designing and teaching in the program. Our collaboration has been a rare privilege—a risky but successful experiment.

Lingering here momentarily, it is natural to wonder if our experience can be replicated within the constraints of more typical academic organizations. I respond with a qualified yes. It would be more difficult, but part of what has made the creation and sustaining of Venture possible is our separate histories of having initiated unusual curriculum innovations or teaching strategies within other colleges and universities. We had all risked, failed, and sometimes succeeded with innovative teaching ideas, learned from our experiences, and found pleasure in these efforts. Together we *expected* to succeed with this project. This belief served us well.

Few of our students had enjoyed this kind of advantage. For them to commit to a full academic year of undergraduate study meant expressing hope in the wake of repeated disappointments and failures—it was evidence of remarkable resilience. This common leap of faith created a deeply felt bond among Venture students.

AMERICAN HISTORY: A MOVING TARGET

By 2005, when I began teaching in Venture, it seemed that everything about our knowledge of American history had changed since I earned my master's degree: the literature had grown in volume and sophistication, historiographical issues had shifted substantially, and, of course, students now had very different questions to ask than they had when I taught history at Clemson University or the University of New Hampshire in the 1960s. For months prior to convening my first Venture class, I immersed myself in the latest research on American history. I thought I had brought myself up to date by the time we commenced our first year of Venture.

The course seemed to work, but it was not because I was ready. It was because the students knew I had jumped into something new as well, and they could sense that, like them, I was gaining new insights as we went along. How utterly different our understanding of Christopher Columbus is today, compared with my education and early teaching. And so it was with our knowledge of slavery, civil rights, American foreign policy, and so many other facets of our history.

Having lived through the intervening decades, I had experienced all these changes, yet I had not truly understood them. As we launched each succeeding year of our Salt Lake City Venture Course, I became more confident of my grasp of American history and savvier about the difficult questions I needed to confront with my students. Still, I wondered what I might have lost because the danger of embarrassment or the prospect of a goofy mistake no longer roiled my gut. Was I still as keenly aware of how some aspects of our history had upset my students' worlds?

A twinge of fright is probably necessary for teaching well anywhere, but so is a looming awareness of our responsibilities to our students and our shared future—a future that is far longer for them than for me. In an age when most lives unfold within, or at the mercy of, massive governmental, corporate, educational, and religious institutions—almost all of them shot full of egregious ethical breaches within their ranks and top echelons—alienation and cynicism are mounting within all age and racial groups and subcultures. Cynicism and fanaticism—opposites that so often spring from the same source—are on the march. Democratic institutions are imperiled by apathy and disenchantment, as well as growing fears, uncertainties, and even hatred at home and around the world.

TEACHING VENTURE STUDENTS IS DIFFERENT

While middle-class students often despair about their world, Venture students tend to see promise. American history looks different to immigrants from an Ebola-stricken part of Africa, refugees from terrorized regions of the Middle East, or someone who has fled from a domestic cult. The United States is a land of hope for them as it may or may not be for a homeless single mother or a newly released prison inmate who receives a Venture scholarship.

Having come from the margins of economic and political systems here and abroad, most Venture students have endured events almost unfathomable to typical college professors, and certainly to me. They have reasons to be angry, alienated, and despairing, and some may begin with these raw edges, but the initiative each of them takes simply to enroll bespeaks a willingness to try again, to reengage. Once the Venture community begins to grow (the seeds seem to germinate at our first rooftop meeting at the downtown library each year), a delicate sense of hope becomes palpable within our group.

This transition comes about in a variety of ways. To illustrate, Ellen only recently escaped from a grueling decade of poverty and vicious physical and emotional abuse. Something had finally snapped inside her, and she sprang free of her marriage—terrified, broken, and exhausted. Her youthful dream of going to college had long since vanished. She forced herself to try again with Venture, but she later described our first few sessions of American history as "one of the most frightening things I ever experienced." She was tentative, uneasy about expressing herself in class, and avoided eye contact with me. One writing assignment—to examine the influence of Abigail Adams on her husband, John Adams—was all it took for me to see gifts that had lain unattended for years. Now my job was to convince her that those talents were still hers.

Teaching American history to my Venture students is quite unlike teaching those in my university courses. Their assets and liabilities are reversed. Most first-year college students have read much but experienced little. In Venture classes, students have often experienced much but read little. They have come to expect the worst, yet they also know they are survivors. When they come to my American history class, they are primed to understand the desperate struggles that so many others across the tapestry of our national life have endured and continue to experience.

My task is to engage Venture students in a way that connects their personal histories with the sweep of American history. How readily my students grasp the meaning of John Lewis's *Walking with the Wind*, the pathos in Dorothea Lange's Depression-era photographs, or the importance of Franklin D. Roosevelt's Works Progress Administration (WPA)—when compared with traditional students in a history course. Yet those other students are more likely to know the works of additional writers about the civil rights movement, to have studied the photography of Jacob Riis, and to be acquainted with other New Deal programs.

Reading the world through alternative spectacles, my Venture students respond uniquely to many history assignments. I require each of them, for example, to spend two hours at the Utah State Capital when the legislature is in session. Students are expected to jot down as many observations as they can about the people, the dynamics, the architecture, and anything else that catches their attention.

What do they see? "A total disconnect between the majestic capitol building and the small-minded and hypocritical discourse inside," Larry reported, "like, whether the first week of February should be declared State Firearms Week?" Another student asked, "Why in the world would the Utah Senate reject a bill to assure basic health and dental care for children in poverty, and then approve an expensive scheme to move the state prison so that wealthy developers can make new fortunes building shopping malls and expensive condos?" He jotted in his journal, "Is this liberty and justice for all?"

At the capitol, Venture students saw mainly old, well-dressed white men in the Senate chamber wrangling over "message bills" about state's rights or Planned Parenthood. Yolanda, while outside on the marble steps, saw people of humble means appeal for Medicaid expansion to help the state's uninsured children. They also noted the fancy cars from which lobbyists emerged, the large number of blue-uniformed law-enforcement personnel, and the lopsided party makeup of the House of Representatives. Odds are my university students would look at the same scene and notice very different things. Subsequent discussions of my Venture students' observations reflected sensitivities and awareness that I want my university students to possess as well. When I point out these discrepancies to my Venture students, we explore the reasons for them and what they mean.

My Venture students' perspectives are accompanied by unusually strong emotions that stem from experiencing police profiling, grinding poverty, capricious violence (especially among refugees), or severe losses. I try to understand their feelings and help them make connections between what they may have experienced and the major events and themes in our nation's history. I want to foster a classroom community in which all students can be authentically who they are, thereby making honest discussions possible.

The challenges Venture students face vary greatly according to the amount of academic experience they bring to the class, the recentness of that education, and their facility with the English language. While these differences are less noticeable as the year progresses, they remain to the end. It is often hard to know how challenging the readings I assign should be. I must avoid overwhelming my less-prepared students, while still pushing the better-grounded ones to their limits. This task is one marked by improvisation, and I still struggle with it every week.

Rarely do Venture students begin with effective conversational skills. Academic discourse that expresses and critiques evidence-based arguments can be quite foreign to them at first. As a result, at the beginning of each semester, I find myself coaching students in the art of listening carefully to one another (and to me). Then I try to teach them how to respond to, or build upon, a previous speaker's point, rather than dart off in a wholly different direction when they get the floor. I struggle to establish good conversational habits within the class, but these skills seem to be acquired more readily and dependably than I anticipated that first year. I am pleasantly surprised each year as I witness their rapid growth.

Classroom challenges, of course, also present opportunities. Because so many of my students have suffered oppression in countries ripped apart by terrorism or war, or have been profiled or mistreated in our country, they identify injustices quickly and readily empathize with those who suffer. This sensitivity makes it easy to engage students in discussions about the American civil rights movement, war crimes, or prison reform. Emotions sometimes overflow—just as they do in standard courses on the Vietnam War or the Iraq wars, which unleash torrential feelings within veterans of those campaigns. Learning to teach in ways that confront the sources of pain and release associated emotions in healthy ways takes time and is my work in progress.

Preoccupation with their issues is frequently where students' engagement with history begins. Early in the course, their writing is egocentric. I don't discourage such expression. But as we go along, examining and applying the enduring ideas that underpin the course, students' perspectives broaden and they begin to see historic events from multiple perspectives. "Six weeks ago," Olga said, "I thought mostly about my problems and felt only the pinch of my issues, but I'm beginning to see things through others' eyes. It's different, you know, like I'm not the only one who matters."

In this way, a concept like justice morphs from being seen as escaping punishment for a dumb mistake or gaining access to a decent job following a stint in prison, to recognizing barriers experienced by whole classes of people who have been denied opportunities for growth or simple dignity. Student imaginations are sparked by the career of Martin Luther King Jr. and the way his life evolved from anger induced by personal affronts to a determination to change a whole system of race and class discrimination by peaceful means.

Indeed, students begin to see that their lives follow similar patterns. "It is as though I can see myself from across the room," Carlos remarked, "and I am just one of many who want a chance to grow. Fairness for me depends on justice for others just as much."

IDEAS THAT INFORM MY VENTURE TEACHING

Teaching American history in Venture, I was reminded how useful Howard Gardner's work on multiple intelligences could be.[3] Human intelligence is not a one-dimensional capacity, as IQ tests presume to measure, but it appears in many forms (verbal, mathematical, musical, spatial, social, physical, etc.) and in almost unlimited permutations. The task is to develop our unique set of intelligences and cluster them to meet the specific opportunities and roles our lives encompass. A consummate basketball player has learned to combine physical/kinesthetic intelligence with spatial, interpersonal, and even intrapersonal intelligences to make the deft pass, shoot the off-balance shot, motivate teammates, or psych out the opposing team. And so it is with the concert pianist, the trial lawyer, or the gifted teacher. Whether the motivation is the passion to survive or the drive to excel, it is the urgency of the task that calls forth the energy and self-discipline to develop and harness the array of skills and intelligences that are essential to mastering anything worthwhile.

As teachers, our job is to catalyze students' minds and motivations in whatever form we encounter them, recognizing that—especially in Venture classrooms—there is surely more genius than initially meets the eye. In a typical classroom setting, the other intelligences are usually expressed through each student's verbal ability. But in my Venture classroom, where verbal intelligence is often masked by unfamiliarity with English, or a lack of language development afforded by reading and writing in good schools, brilliance in other intelligences can be especially difficult to identify and cultivate.

To illustrate, every teacher knows what it is like to listen to a student make an earnest comment in class, then have no clue what he or she has just said. After the "could you elaborate on that?" suggestion, there is still no comprehension. Looking around, I see that the other students also appear to be in the dark. No help there. Sometimes the issue is muddled thinking, but more often than not with Venture students, language is the problem. Within a class of twenty-five, six or more first languages may lie behind newly embraced English. Russian, Portuguese, Spanish, Farsi, Navajo, and Swahili—all in one class. Another mix of languages may be present the next year.

I try earnestly to comprehend every comment, but sometimes I can mutter only a faintly upbeat, "Thank you, Emilio," and then seek the student out after class to make a more intense exploration of his or her meaning. Their frustrations may have escaped my awareness, but in most cases, we come to understand each other and establish rapport in the process. Still, these incidents produce some of my most stressful moments in class because I know there is insight I am missing and potential I cannot unlock.

If my students' verbal intelligence is sometimes masked by lack of sophistication in the English language, their brilliance in other realms may also pass my notice. Interpersonal and intrapersonal intelligences are sometimes exquisitely expressed in cultures and subcultures foreign to my experience and therefore beyond my comprehension or appreciation. The same may be true of musical or artistic intelligences, where I am unlikely to see and recognize high achievement due to students' reticence to share what they do or have done in cultural settings more natural to them. "What genius am I not able to see," I often ask myself, and then suddenly, in a spontaneous gesture, that student or another brings a musical instrument to class and stuns us all with a solo performance to illustrate a recent discussion.

Turning from factors bearing on teaching our students to those that may be characteristic of Venture faculty members, what personal qualities may make Venture professors especially effective teachers? If some can be identified, how can they inform the selection and development of Venture faculty members?

In my prior service as dean of liberal education at the University of Utah, I sought out the most able teachers and enlisted them through release time to serve as faculty in our core liberal-education classes that were required for all students. Then, working with those who excelled in this program over a period of years, I identified ten professors from across our sprawling campus who were rated among the best on student course evaluations or most often cited by graduating seniors as having made the greatest difference in their education at the university. These two methods of identifying unusually effective teaching produced the same names only about half the time. My group of ten was drawn from professors who rose to the top according to both criteria.

Wondering what these colleagues might have in common, I invited each one to lunch at a café close to campus. We engaged in a conversation that I guided as subtly as possible using a series of questions about their teaching philosophies, life experiences, and personal beliefs. My work was aided or impeded—as one might judge—by knowing almost all of these scholars, some very well. Even so, when I look back over the series of conversations, some surprising conclusions pop out that seem particularly useful in relation to Venture teaching.

My consensus teaching stars were united in regarding each student as a valuable human being who had important things to offer others. Neither a vessel to be filled nor a subject to be served, every student was to them inherently interesting and worthy of attention and encouragement. Similarly, these teachers believed the ideas and information they taught were fundamentally important for their students to understand and potentially useful for their futures—as well as for society. If most teachers fall into one of two groups—those who teach students and those who teach subject matter—these professors straddled the divide and kept the two sides of this equation in balance.

Perhaps for this reason, the faculty standouts I interviewed exhibited two other characteristics in common. Reflecting John Dewey's tenet that "education is not preparation for life; it is life itself," they regarded teaching as the most real of experiences. It was never a game to be played with a pea and three shells—with put-downs or one-ups—nor a test of authority, will, or status. As a result, these teachers were authentic and real in the classroom and outside it—natural, approachable, and unthreatening. They were all mavericks by nature, resisting professorial affectations and socially defined expectations and embracing the out-of-the-ordinary in both experience and taste.

Looking further at personal characteristics, I can see these gifted teachers lived comfortably on the margin between theory and practice, between established ways and emergent ideas, and between individual standards and community values. Rather than eschew ambiguity, they seemed to welcome situations brimming with it and, thus, empathized genuinely with students whose cultures, values, and lifeways presented conflicts with prevailing social norms.

These teachers did not offer answers because they did not believe their teaching was about answers. For them, great questions about knowledge, truth, and goodness remained as intriguing and important as they had been in their undergraduate years or when they had launched their teaching careers. Little wonder that they embraced each new class with the enthusiasm of potential discovery. They were still learning, and the less orthodox their students, the more likely a fresh question or new insight might appear. Knowing what I had learned from these interviews, it became clear to me that teaching American history to Venture students would enhance my growth in fruitful ways.

THE CORE OF MY VENTURE PEDAGOGY

Teaching American history with an emphasis on the ebb and flow of liberty and justice in our society made it incumbent upon me to use every natural opening to model democratic values. Discussing and trying to practice Walt Whitman's notion of a "spiritual democracy" gave me the perfect opening.[4] I was drawn instinctively to his notion that if I choose to regard every person I meet as my equal, I have created and live within my own egalitarian republic. To the extent that this ethic of valuing others as equals becomes the norm within our classrooms, our institutions, and the whole body politic, our separate republics-in-spirit will merge and invigorate the tangible political democracy for which people yearn the world around.

I believe Whitman's notion of a personal democracy is the necessary precondition of political and intellectual freedom. The wellspring of democracy rests within the heart and mind of individual students, professors, and citizens. Our fragile experiment with democracy in America, therefore, is poised precariously on the most intangible element of our existence: my conscience and that of others. I know of no educational setting other than the Venture classroom where Whitman's concept has greater power.

One way I promote an expectation of engagement with society through teaching history to Venture students is to design writing assignments that require it. With a paper due every other week, I have found that students respond favorably to the challenge of making real arguments.

Instead of assigning several pages on the causes of the Civil War, for example, I ask that they envision themselves in 1862 and then write a letter to President Lincoln with their plan to resolve the growing North-South tensions peacefully. Or, similarly, I ask students to assume they are in college in 1960 and they must write a letter to a friend explaining why they believe Richard Nixon would make a better president than John Kennedy. I want to force students to make a counterintuitive argument in the light of their awareness of Kennedy's subsequent popularity.

These assignments lead to others that require students to use their growing historical knowledge to explain their positions on current domestic or foreign policy issues. They must write and mail a letter to a U.S. senator or member of Congress from Utah urging him or her to vote a certain way on an emerging bill. Alternatively they can write a letter to the editor of the *Salt Lake Tribune*. Over the last seven years, several students have had their letters published, and others have had their letters to members of Congress respectfully acknowledged or read into the *Congressional Record*.

Because they have tasted such rewards, or observed a classmate who has succeeded, it is not a stretch to imagine that Venture alumni will continue to express their views publicly. In the words of biographer Park Honan, such a practice "begins to dispel any passive attitude toward life, by which responsibility is allowed to go by default to those who always stand ready to seize it unworthily."[5]

To encourage habits of careful argumentation and public engagement, I have pondered how I can best quicken my students' consciences—their capacity to hold self-interest in check and suspend the destructive facets of ego expression. Every wisdom tradition and great religion has hallowed a few enduring ideals, and a surprising number of them are shared across cultures and traditions. Mortimer Adler wrote about six great ideas—too few by about half, by my reckoning—which he grouped by western cultures (his intellectual bailiwick).[6] Three were central to Greek culture: *goodness, truth,* and *beauty.* And the French Revolution celebrated three others: *liberty, equality,* and *fraternity.* To these six, I believe we must add at least *justice* and *mercy* from the sacred texts of Judaism, Christianity, and Islam.

These honorable ideals, when understood and internalized, can change the way Venture students see themselves and understand those around them. But not necessarily. Students can study multiple theories of justice, master tomes on just laws and unjust wars, and write essays on historical figures who mustered the courage to act justly, but there is little evidence that any of this intellectual work prompts them (or us) to behave in a more humane or courageous manner. That crucial step requires empathy—earned through engaging in real experience with others. That empathy encourages reflective reasoning and quickens their capacity to understand the feelings, motivations, and intentions of those around them.

I understood the difference between theorizing and empathizing as never before while attending an Aspen Institute Justice and Society Seminar.

On a weekend break with a fellow student, I found myself pumping gas into my old blue Explorer at the Diamond Station on nearby Leadville's forlorn main street. I glanced up to see two Harley-Davidson riders urinating on mine tailings just a few feet beyond the pumps. Having completed their task, they stepped inside to pay for their fuel.

My Australian friend and coparticipant in the Aspen seminar, David Stockley, remarked as we proceeded up the heavily pitted street, "Leadville is impoverished and depressing, but it is as important to see this sorry town as it is to see glittering Aspen." Our afternoon venture across Colorado's lofty Independence Pass, of course, was not in the curriculum, but it should have been.

The trouble with the Justice and Society Seminar was that it seemed all Aspen and no Leadville. As individuals and as a society, our problem is rarely whether to be just or unjust because most people strive to do right by others most of the time. Rather, the question is whether we can *feel* what others' daily lives are like and truly understand the issues they face. Until we gain this awareness, we cannot temper our self-interest, balance competing ideals such as liberty and justice, and know what doing justly requires of us.

In one sense, of course, our posh seminar was a quest for these balances. But in others, it was not. We were an overwhelmingly privileged assemblage—analytically intense, theoretically oriented, and socially and economically secure. In our formal sessions, we were all mind and no heart. Well meaning, certainly, but bloodless.

To affect behavior, an idea or ideal must penetrate our rational minds and lay a claim on our consciences. Once our hearts get involved along with our intellects, everything can change, usually (although not always) for the better. I have seen this principle at work in my Venture students. Minds as different as Thomas Merton, Abraham Maslow, and Ralph Waldo Emerson described this transformation in surprisingly similar terms.[7] The highest purpose of education is to prepare each student for ignition by establishing the conditions and providing the materials that make flashes of insight possible.

Learning is not a gradual progression. In clearer terms, it is characterized by long periods of absorption—often tedious and frustrating—leading up to peak moments of discovery. Clearly teachers vary in their ability to set the conditions and provide the materials that predispose others for their leaps of insight, but these moments seem to happen in my Venture classroom almost without me. My American history students are not competing for academic knowledge; they are striving to change their lives, and every reading or new idea is examined with corresponding earnestness.

If William Perry got it right years ago in his groundbreaking study of the interrelated nature of intellectual and ethical development among Harvard students, then "setting the conditions" goes well beyond making wise and challenging assignments and providing an unthreatening environment to explore ideas and consider their implications.[8] His research made it clear that in so much of college teaching, professors are inaccessible to students as whole human beings. The student-faculty dynamic inherent in Venture courses—involving teaching and mentoring and the direct application of learning to life—naturally provides Perry's missing element.

If this happy observation is true, then it matters to Venture students that their teachers struggle to live the ideals we teach. What promises to change our students' behavior is witnessing a just act by someone they admire, seeing a merciful gesture (or benefitting from one), or absorbing the beauty of something both good and wholly unanticipated. It helps if a humanities professor's way of being reflects the ideas and ideals she or he teaches, though we all fall painfully short. Beyond the virtues we can model, each of us has the capacity to bring students into contact with other people who are exemplars of integrity, especially through the historical writing and creative literature we ask them to read and discuss.

Perry made clear, however, that there are perils if students know only one person who exemplifies mature ethical living and democratic virtues. Knowing just one person can be intimidating because the student may infer that having a satisfying life is possible only by living that particular way. Since none of us can become the same as another person, even if we wish to be, then relating positively to a single mentor creates a problem.

What I try to provide every Venture student in American history, therefore, is access to—or at least an awareness of—a variety of healthy models—from teachers, friends, and associates in Venture to the lives of historical figures—who cleave to different combinations of noble ideas. This broad approach leaves them the option of choosing their own paths while borrowing freely from the fine qualities they observe in others.

The personal models Perry believed are so vital to our development need not be living—or even real—people. But they must be believable and engaging. The annals of history and literature are chockful of such figures. Historians often describe their challenges and conflicts, their tragedies and triumphs, in gripping detail. Further, novelists create characters that inspire, disgust, and inform us with their humanity and inhumanity. All these characters can serve as touchstones against which Venture students may strike their own actions and measure their own integrity.

Historian Howard Zinn's *A People's History of the United States* provides a valuable compendium of stories about many of our overlooked or forgotten forbearers.[9] My Venture students are often shocked by the mistakes and failures of our national heroes—as Zinn describes their lives, achievements, and soft underbellies. But they soon come to appreciate how deeply we are all caught in the paradoxes of our times and blinded by the confines of our cultures, and how difficult it is to see beyond these limitations and live by more universal values.

Knowing others' imperfections empowers us to accept our weaknesses and provides a stimulus to rise above them. Similarly, Zinn's passion to illuminate the struggles and occasional triumphs of the ordinary and the oppressed provides the gift of new models and new heroes while shrinking the distance between ourselves and those we hold in high regard.

Which of the many historical characters in Zinn's book, or those who appear in historically anchored articles I choose from the *New York Review of Books*, best informs a student's own struggles and aspirations? The set is undoubtedly different for each person, of course, but vigorously discussing any of them enables students to become comfortable sharing their aspirations, passions, and personal challenges.

Many works of American history illuminate the complex relationships among the world's enduring ideas. An American conservative's opposition to EPA emission standards for industry or vehicles (in the name of freedom) runs headlong into a liberal's passion for clean air for all to breathe (in the name of equality). The more we seek liberty, the less room remains for equality. The greater our demand for justice in a criminal case, the less we satisfy our love for mercy. And vice versa. Single-minded loyalty to any great idea inevitably demands that others give way in a comparable amount.

SUMMING UP

Teaching American history in Venture, I relish the opportunity to compare the unresolved issues of our national life—from racism, religious bigotry, ideological rigidity, and economic imperialism—with our nation's founding ideals, among them the American mantra of "liberty and justice for all." I also hope that my students will understand that when reasonable balance is lost because the pendulum swings too far right or left, the consequences can be catastrophic. Injustice and lack of mercy strike whole swaths of the population. Alienation abounds. Unhealthy conditions prevail.

Here and abroad, a disproportionate number of Venture students' experiences have involved unhealthy institutions, individuals, and governments. Many of them have never lived without fear, had reason to trust anyone in authority, or known the security and happiness of living within an embracing family or community.

Ashaki, for instance, has survived the terrors of genocide in Africa, the privations of refugee camps, and the challenge of starting anew in a culture utterly baffling to her. She spoke no English before arriving in Salt Lake City. One of Ashaki's classmates almost missed class one evening because all four tires on her old van had been slashed. The story of her self-liberation from a southern Utah polygamous community had appeared in the city newspapers that morning. While such experiences destroy many, some, like these students, somehow endure. They are the exceptions that—by teaching American history honestly—I dream of making the norm.

For the first time, these students have come to understand America's experiment with government of the people and by the people from the point of view of its ideals and controlling ideas. Both of these have been contradicted and betrayed, but they also make this country unique because they continue to inspire people here and around the world. I hope to give my students a sense of what makes the country different and encourage them to care about its future by getting involved in the political process. I want them to know not only that they belong *in* America, but that they also belong *to* America. And America belongs to them.

NOTES

1.   L. Jackson Newell, *The Electric Edge of Academe: The Saga of Lucien L. Nunn and Deep Springs College* (Salt Lake City: University of Utah Press, 2015).

2. Paulo Freire, *Pedagogy of Freedom: Ethics, Democracy, and Civic Courage* (Lanham, MD: Rowman & Littlefield, 1998), 31.

3. Howard Gardner, *Frames of Mind: The Theory of Multiple Intelligences* (New York: Basic Books, 1983).

4. Walt Whitman, *Democratic Vistas: And Other Papers* (London and Toronto: W. J. Gage & Co., 1888), 27.

5. Newell, *The Electric Edge of Academe,* xv.

6. Mortimer J. Adler, *Six Great Ideas* (New York: Touchstone Books, 1997).

7. See Thomas Merton's essay, "Learning to Live," in *Love and Living,* ed. Naomi B. Stone and Brother Patrick Hart (San Diego: Harvest/HBJ, 1985); chapter 11 in Abraham H. Maslow, *Motivation and Personality* (New York: Harper & Row, 1954); and Ralph Waldo Emerson's essay, "The American Scholar," in *Selected Essays* (New York: Penguin Books, 1982).

8. William G. Perry Jr., *Forms of Intellectual and Ethical Development in the College Years: A Scheme* (New York: Holt, Rinehart and Winston, 1970).

9. Howard Zinn, *A People's History of the United States* (New York: Harper & Row, 1980).

8

CHALLENGES

JEFF METCALF

I noticed students who didn't complete assignments, and the professors didn't seem to mind. I think they should be honest [about academic demands in college] and expect more out of the students.

—VENTURE GRADUATE, *FROM AN ANONYMOUS ONLINE SURVEY*

When we started Venture, we thought we understood the difficulties students might have navigating the course, and much of what we imagined might happen, did. Some became ill or a family member became incapacitated, and they had to leave the course to provide care. Or the work became too difficult and their poor academic preparation made the challenge of Venture too frustrating. Family responsibilities interfered with coming to class, and they had to miss too many evenings, discouraging them from finishing. Others moved away to get better employment.

But we didn't anticipate the long reach of poverty. Sometimes a student's reason for withdrawing was the chance to change work hours for a dollar-an-hour raise. That counts when it means putting food on the table.

The loss of students from the course can be heartbreaking. "It's distressing, especially when you don't think they'll find their way back to the classroom," says Jean Cheney. "I've had students drop out of my college classes and hardly noticed. When they drop out of Venture, especially after a few months, it's devastating." This is not to suggest that losing a student from a college class isn't also felt, but its significance is different. In all probability, students in their teens or early twenties make it back into a classroom. Our students are rarely in their twenties and—as in the case with Drew—we must acknowledge that a return to higher learning later in their lives will probably not be an option. He wrote us the following e-mail:

> I want to start out by thanking you for such wonderful learning experiences with my time in Venture. The atmosphere and attitude have been incredibly conducive for deeper learning and discovering a better me. This program has been a treasure in my life that has forever bettered the person I am.
>
> You might be wondering what the purpose of this e-mail is…unfortunately, it comes with sad emotion. My work has provided an opportunity for me to travel while gaining an increase in pay. It is with a heavy heart that I have to say good-bye to the Venture program. My schedule at work won't permit me to attend Venture. I have thoroughly enjoyed the professors and their love for learning, as well as this entire program.
>
> Thank you again for a life-changing experience with the Venture Course in the Humanities!

Did Drew make the right choice for his future? At the time he left Venture, we thought he would never find his way back to higher education. That is often the case. But in Drew's situation, our prediction was wrong—happily and completely. Just before going to press with this book, we received a pleasantly surprising e-mail.[1]

Venture students must commit to a full academic year. We don't advertise the program as a semester-long course. In our embryonic beginnings, if a student dropped, we did not fill the opening. But as we began to see openings occurring year after year, we decided it made little sense to leave those spots vacant when we had people eager to start Venture. It seemed logical, if we had openings, to allow students to join the course at the semester break. We began accepting a few new students each January.

To address the issue of students who had to drop the course but wanted to return when their situation changed, we created an open-door policy that allowed them to reapply. A number of Venture students have returned under this policy and have done remarkably well. Unfortunately, however, once students drop the course, they usually don't return.

To help reduce student attrition, our roles as teachers extend beyond the subjects we teach. Venture students bond quickly to each other and to their teachers and often share their worries in conversations before and after class and during the break. When we learn about problems students are having, we often take time at the beginning of the next class to make announcements that relate to the issue they have raised. We mention job possibilities, tutorial services, child-friendly activities, income-tax-preparation seminars, extended hours at a free health clinic, housing and legal counsel.

Women outnumber men every year in Venture, often two or three to one, and the pressures on them are especially great. Many are single-income mothers, the sole providers for their children. When appropriate, we encourage them to connect with family members or friends to share responsibilities, and many of them do, especially when emergencies arise, such as having to care for a sick child.

Financial stress affects all of our students, often making it difficult to focus on their studies. We are aware that finding time for Venture is a challenge that each student must resolve, usually during the fall semester. From the first meeting at orientation, we let students know that we recognize the difficulties they may face in Venture. We refer to previous classes that have wrestled with these same stressors and make it clear that if, for any reason, they can't continue with the class, they should not consider that a failure. Unfortunately, sometimes life gets in the way.

If you grow up poor in America, you are likely to have attended a substandard school and often lack good reading and writing skills and study habits. It's impossible in a two-semester program to make up for this inadequate education. When Venture students are refugees or recent immigrants, they also wrestle with English as a second language.

Students at a community college or university usually begin with a similar set of academic tools. Venture students do not. Some of our students haven't graduated from high school or are concurrently working on their GEDs. Some graduated from inner-city or rural schools with limited resources; others went to decent schools and did well. Some finished high school outside this country and may or may not have had much exposure to the English language or the humanities. Others learned English after coming to the U.S. as children or teenagers and are fluent orally, with a strong command of grammar and vocabulary, but struggle with writing. As a result of these varied backgrounds, some Venture students are strong readers; others read word for word. Some write well; others have trouble constructing a clear sentence.

Thus, in every Venture class, we have a few students capable of college work, several barely prepared, and a few totally unprepared. How do we design a curriculum to address all of their needs? We've struggled with this issue since the beginning of Venture. What strengths can we build upon? How do we do the very best by our students in an incredibly short period of time? How do we engage our students without concentrating on patching up a system that has continually failed them? How do we make right what is wrong?

We have students eager to be included in the world who have made a brave and bold move to be counted. By enrolling in Venture, we hear them saying, "I will do everything in my power to better myself through education because it is the most important thing I can do for me and my family." We can't turn back the clock, but we can meet them where they are and begin from that point to create a discourse that includes their voices and ideas in the most meaningful way possible.

Venture has evolved over the years. We've learned to adapt, to find partnerships in the community willing to support and work with our students. Writing mentors from the Community Writing Center, part of Salt Lake Community College's outreach, provide tutorial services for Venture students before class. University of Utah students, learning to become teachers, help lead small groups in the classroom and provide one-on-one teaching during Venture's two-hour classes. This experience also models an open-ended, discussion approach to humanities education for these aspiring teachers with the hope that they will, in turn, realize the power of that approach in their classrooms.

One of the most difficult problems we have faced as a faculty is how to grade our students at the end of each semester. Westminster College grants four hours of college credit each semester to students in Venture who pass, and eight hours for both semesters. The students must pass all five of the disciplines in the humanities to receive this credit. But when we pass a Venture student, are we certifying that she or he has completed college-level work? Should we pass a student whose writing might not receive a passing grade in a college class or whose reading comprehension may be low but who participates actively in class and shows definite understanding of course content?

We hear from other Clemente course directors and instructors that there is a wide difference of opinion nationally on how to grade, evaluate, and respond to student work in the classes. Some fervently believe that they are doing a tremendous disservice to students if they pass an essay that wouldn't earn at least a C grade in most university writing classes. Others demur: Why insist on evidence of learning only through writing when some students reveal advanced comprehension through oral participation?

Wrestling with these questions, we have tried to keep in mind that the Venture Course, like Clemente courses throughout the country, is not designed to prepare students for college or university. It aims to empower students and open possibilities for them, however they define those possibilities. It encourages engagement in their communities and with the larger world. If a student wants to continue his or her education, we support that desire in any way we can. In fact, more than half of our Venture students do continue formal education after the program, getting their GED equivalency diplomas, attending community college, or applying for and often getting scholarships to state and private universities. A few have gone on to graduate school to earn advanced degrees.

In our teaching and student assessments, we seek a balance between keeping standards as clear and high as possible and still meeting the needs of the range of academic abilities in our classes. We find a variety of ways to assess learning. We emphasize showing up, whether a student has completed the homework or not. We don't want students to miss the benefit of class discussion and learning. But we recognize that we can't always accommodate all students, particularly those already working on a college level. An anonymous response on an online survey from one Venture graduate makes this clear:

> I loved the Venture course because I was considering going back to school for the first time in over ten years, and I was very nervous about it. I enrolled at Weber State, and I am planning on

continuing my education to become a nurse. The only criticism I can give the program is that it was not like most college classes. I noticed many students who didn't complete assignments or do the assigned readings, and the professors didn't mind. I know this course is designed to get people back into the swing of things and to prepare them for further education, but I think the professors should be honest and expect more out of the students.

Whether the accommodation to students described here supports or undermines student progress is up to their teachers to decide. Each professor chooses the way to evaluate learning in his or her class. In spite of diverse opinions about evaluation among our faculty members, we have found surprising agreement regarding who should receive credit for the course and who should not at the end of the semester. Students who attend the requisite number of classes, but whose work does not earn a passing grade, receive a certificate of achievement but not college credit.

More relevant to the goal of Venture than college credit is whether or not students have become engaged citizens. Are graduates more involved in their communities? Do they vote, write letters to the editor, attend parent meetings at their children's school, and involve themselves in their church or neighborhood community groups? Do they pay attention to the news and believe they have a voice—and responsibility—to the world outside of themselves? Do they continue to enjoy learning and participate in cultural activities after the course is over? We have some evidence—through end-of-year and follow-up surveys—that the answer to all of these questions is a qualified yes.

To be able to discuss Socrates's notion of the unexamined life, see parallels between Sophocles's *Antigone* and the modern world, wrestle with Harper Lee's issues of race and prejudice in *To Kill a Mockingbird*, see the influences of history in architecture, and know American history and understand how delicate is our experiment in democracy—these are marvelous accomplishments by anyone's standards. Our students leave the course with their minds awake. The world has become a more interesting place, and they are eager to take their place in it. The challenges they—and we—encounter pale in comparison with these triumphs.

NOTES

1. Here is the text of Drew's e-mail:

> Hello!
>
> It's been a long time since having been with you in the Venture program. I remember the incredible discussions and creative opportunities I had while venturing with you and so many others. I find myself looking back with fond memories of the jump start it gave me to my college pursuits.
>
> I'm happy to announce that I'll be graduating this October from Ashford University in San Diego from the Ashford University Forbes School of Business in PR and Marketing. What a journey it has been!
>
> I'm reaching out to let you know how grateful I am for the Venture program. Bringing people together from so many diverse backgrounds helped me to branch out and finish my pursuit of secondary [higher] education.
>
> Hope you are doing well. I look forward to hearing from you.
>
> Drew

GOING PUBLIC

Venture Students Speak

JEAN CHENEY

Do we continue to tell ourselves that people in prison have chosen their own path in life; it's their own problem that they're losers? If people are put back on the street the exact same way they were (or worse) when they went into prison, things will never change. Venture did something for me that is difficult to put into words. I think now. I read now. I still don't speak well, but I THINK NOW.

—LISA DEHERRERA, *VENTURE GRADUATE*

THE VENTURE EXHIBIT

During the winter of 2006, the first year of the Venture Course in Utah, a documentary photographer in Salt Lake City approached the faculty with an idea. Kent Miles often works with oral historians to create exhibits and books featuring stories that have been missing from the record. In fact, on the fourth floor at Horizonte, near the library where we held Venture classes, the walls are lined with striking black-and-white portraits of

Horizonte graduates, all taken by Kent. Below each face is a personal state-ment in the student's handwriting. As we headed to the library for class each Tuesday and Thursday night, we passed these portraits. Their faces and stories are part of the place we inhabited. As they walked by, our stu-dents sometimes stop and gaze at men and women who look like them and read their stories.

Kent had heard about the Venture Course and sent us an e-mail: Had we thought about doing an exhibit featuring student work? Had we considered sharing their voices with the community? He thought news of the course was important to share and offered to take the students' portraits at cost.

His idea intrigued us. What if we invited our students to tell their sto-ries and share the assignments they had been completing in Venture? How might this boost their self-confidence and engagement in their communi-ties? The faculty met with Kent to hear more about his proposal. For an exhibit showcasing Venture and the students' work, he suggested creat-ing a separate panel for each student with a black-and-white portrait and a sample of his or her writing.

Pulling together an exhibit of these panels would bring Venture out of the classroom into a public space. He suggested that the exhibit be shown in Salt Lake's downtown library, where we hold orientation. In 2006, the library was a stunning new structure, attracting a lot of attention with its five-story, open-air Urban Room that was like a glass-enclosed city street. On the lower level of that room was an intimate exhibit space, specifi-cally designed for community work. After being shown at the downtown library, the Venture exhibit could go to other libraries or community cen-ters, spreading the word about the course, extending the impact of our stu-dents' work and voices, and helping us recruit new students.

But wait. Our students had not shared their stories or written their essays for public consumption. By the time Kent approached us, students in this first Venture Course had become a close-knit community that was based on trust and held together by affection and respect. Students regarded Venture as a safe zone. What they said to each other, they said in confi-dence. They knew they would not be judged by what they had done in the past or what had been done to them. We encouraged, but never required, that they share their writing with each other or with us, but they almost always did, even if it meant passing tissues or sitting together in long, heavy silences. We certainly had never planned on sharing in public what had been happening within the library at Horizonte. That violated a compact we had made. Urging them to exhibit their work in public felt like exploitation.

At a second meeting, we told Kent that we didn't want to expose our students or their work to public scrutiny. That betrayed, on a deep level, the trust they had placed in us. We didn't want to jeopardize what we and the students had built together; nothing was worth that. Our students were proud people with personal dignity we greatly respected.

Kent listened, then asked,

Have you considered what the students might gain as a result of sharing their work more broadly? Might they take pride in their academic achievement? Might they want their faces and their stories associated with this effort? Might this give them—for maybe the first time in their lives—a public forum for their ideas? Would they enjoy knowing that others might benefit from reading their work?

Kent's good questions created a quandary for us. As we eventually learned to do with all important questions about Venture, we decided to ask the students. They would decide. Before we broached the specific question of the exhibit, however, we told them that we were neutral about the question we were posing. We saw value in the idea but also potential threat. We were interested in what they thought.

The discussion showed us how much we had underestimated our students or, perhaps, misunderstood them. They were immediately excited about the exhibit. They liked the idea of showcasing their work. Had they thought about what it would feel like to have their names, faces, personal stories, and work available to strangers, we asked? The introductory panel at the exhibit would describe Venture as a free humanities course for people living on low incomes. Were they comfortable with that explanation? A few agreed that they were taking a risk, but even those students said that it would be "worth it." They wanted to "go public."

"We can control what gets displayed, right?" a few asked.

We assured them that they could and would. Nothing would be exhibited without their consent. "Let's do it!" They were unanimous. To have a public way of sharing what had intrigued them in the course—what they had learned and how their learning had affected them—was thrilling, they thought.

We had overblown our worries. We had not understood the pride our students took in their work and sharing their voices. How eager they were! Although they didn't put it this way, it was as if they didn't want their missing stories to be missing any longer. They wanted to bring their words, their ideas, and their lives into the public arena.

Together we decided that each panel in the exhibit would have three components: the student's portrait, an introduction to the student written by a classmate, and a sample of the student's work taken from a course assignment. We would build the exhibit together. Students would submit the work they wanted to include. As their writing teacher, Jean would help them edit the piece if it was too long. The student would approve all the writing that appeared on his or her panel, including the introduction by a classmate. We would work to ensure that writing from assignments in all five disciplines was represented.

After viewing the panels, a visitor would understand that Venture was an academic course but something more: an encounter with philosophical ideas and a place to grow; an examination of history, literature, and art, and a passage; an engagement that opened minds and emboldened hearts.

With Kent Miles's help and the students' hard work, we created the exhibit that spring. "Transformations through the Humanities" was shown in June 2006 in the downtown Salt Lake City Library at an opening attended by Venture students, their families and friends, and supporters of Westminster College, Horizonte, and UHC. After several months there, the exhibit traveled to two other city libraries, a county library, and two community centers. The photographs were also featured in an article about Venture in *Humanities*, a magazine published by the National Endowment for the Humanities.

We estimate that the exhibit allowed thousands of people to read Venture students' words and study their expressive faces, captured by Kent on black-and-white film. At the opening, our students mixed with people they had never met and listened to their comments as they studied the panels. Their faces were alive with pride. Following are samples of photos and panels from this exhibit.

GINA ZIVKOVIC BY BARBRA MOELLER
When you have known pain and sorrow you can run from it, or become it. Gina ran toward it. Tempting danger makes one feel stronger. One day, however,

Gina Zivkovic, 2005. Photo courtesy of Kent Miles; used with permission.

she realized that she had broken free from those who abused her only to replace outward blows with inner turmoil, drugs, and neglect. Eventually, she let her mistakes become the fertilizer of experience, becoming a professional gardener. Through courage, hard work, and a faith in Christ that humbles me, my friend Gina has grown into a whole, complete, amazing woman.

GINA ZIVKOVIC

Ranch life for Gretel Ehrlich in "The Solace of Open Spaces" was physically demanding, requiring self-reliance, vigor, and common sense. But the solitude also created quiet, providing a richness of thought and feeling for which there is no vocabulary. As Ehrlich describes it, "The silence is profound. Instead of talking, we seem to share one eye. . . . Days unfold, bathed in their own music."

My family relishes any opportunity to escape the congestion, blaring noise, and growing restriction of urban living. The mindless streams of traffic, miles and miles of pavement and sidewalk, stench of exhaust and fumes press down on us. Wires and poles of all shapes and sizes confuse the sky. At night, streetlights and billboards choke out the stars. Sirens wail and motors roar at all hours of the day, and throngs of people seethe in and out. Our space is full of noise, stench, and clutter. The beauty, peace, simplicity, and solitude of the natural land have been eaten to give room for our human quest for more.

Barbra Moeller, 2005. Photo courtesy of Kent Miles; used with permission.

EARLEEN RICHARDSON BY DOT RICHEDA

Earleen is a beautiful name for a beautiful lady. When we met, Earleen was a shy person, but through our classes each week, she has become more confident. She enjoys reading Ivan Doig, Wallace Stegner, and Terry Tempest Williams. During the year, we attended the Salgado exhibit, heard jazz music, and visited the Utah Museum of Fine Arts together. Earleen is not a name but my FRIEND for life.

EARLEEN RICHARDSON

The art of releasing a body from a piece of rock is no small accomplishment: Michelangelo's work is truly miraculous. The details shown in every inch of *David*'s body require a thorough knowledge of anatomy. The whole work had to have been envisioned before beginning: the stone is not forgiving of errors or lack of foresight. Balance is present, and contrapposto is used well to represent the immediate action that will be required by David. Besides the skill that is necessary to create the physical reality of this biblical character, the sculptor also captures the psychological stress of the situation. Michelangelo's awareness of the latter element creates an unforgettable portrayal.

DOT RICHEDA BY EARLEEN RICHARDSON

Dot is a bundle of energy in a small package. She asks lots of questions, and if she feels the need to speak, she does so without hesitation. "I thought that was very interesting" is a comment she makes frequently. Her warmth and concern for others are evident by her hugs. Although Dot was raised in a traditional Japanese home, she is far from traditional now. She will never walk three steps behind any man!

DOT RICHEDA

In 1955, before the monument was built over the *USS Arizona,* I had the opportunity to visit the site. It had a simple flagpole attached to the broken main mast of the ship with a commemorative plaque. While riding the transport over to the platform, I felt a somber peace come over me. This was the final resting place for members of the *USS Arizona.* I could still see oil spots coming up from the sunken ship every few minutes.

I can only imagine what happened on that fateful day, December 7, 1941. Planes flying, bombs, sailors trapped in their ships. Some of the

Lisa DeHerrera, 2005. Photo courtesy of Kent Miles; used with permission.

men trapped in the *Arizona* tapped Morse code to let the rescuers know they were still alive. These men were never rescued and are entombed in the ship. They never had the opportunity to go to college or have a family.

I treasure the men and women who lost their lives that day, giving us the liberty to live happy and worthy lives. After moving away from Hawaii, I became aware of other issues related to liberty in history—slavery, civil rights, the Holocaust, Japanese internment camps, and many other persecutions around the world. As a member of JACL (Japanese American Citizens League), the oldest civil rights group in America, I have worked to protect our rights and liberty, precious gifts of freedom we should never take lightly.

SILVIA FACIO BY GINA ZIVKOVIC
At age six, Silvia lost her mother to untreated breast cancer. In Zacatecas, Mexico, there is little chance to obtain health care. After her mother's death,

she quietly put aside her little girl things and joined her two brothers in soccer, basketball, and wrestling, becoming very independent. In 1996, at fourteen, Silvia and her family moved from Mexico to Salt Lake City. Her dream today is to study astronomy and become an astronaut.

SILVIA FACIO

For the final paper in art history class, our professor asked us to write a paper about an important building that reflected a part of history that we had learned about. I chose the Cathedral of the Madeleine. It took me almost a month to write this paper. I went to the church myself to write. I took my book with me. I started to remember what the teacher told us about research. I started to recognize all the paintings, the structure of the building, the materials used to build this amazing cathedral. I started to recognize the style of the paintings—Gothic, Roman, Greek, etc. I spent more than three hours in the church, writing. I used a lot of paper that ended up in the garbage. The more I wrote, the more I remembered how to do it, and I got more confident about it. I described the whole church from inside. That paper is my first baby. I grew up with it. I took care of it. I developed myself while I wrote it. This paper was the hardest paper I did that semester, but it strengthened my knowledge about art history.

MINDY CLARK BY LISA DEHERRERA

Mindy doesn't see people's characteristics in black and white; she sees various shades of gray. She has a keen sense of who a person is and what may have molded them into who they are. Mindy is compassionate in her acceptance of others without compromising her own values and morals. What I've enjoyed most about Mindy is her genuineness of character, easy laugh, and sincere friendship.

MINDY CLARK

Socrates believed he was a victim of men, not of laws. He believed that if a person has been born into a community, raised by the community, and schooled by the community, that person has an obligation to abide by the laws of the community. If a person feels a law unjust, it is his right to either convince the state of the injustice or, when he comes of age, leave the community. He says, "Now you depart in innocence, a sufferer and not a doer of evil; a victim, not of the laws, but of men." So you see, when

Steven Acevedo, 2005. Photo courtesy of Kent Miles; used with permission.

he was sentenced to die, it is not the laws that have betrayed Socrates but the men who used the laws to their own advantage to rid themselves from any further embarrassment caused by him. The reasons Socrates gives for not escaping make perfect sense and are made not with his emotions (as most of us tend to do) but with sound logic. I think that if everyone applied Socrates's philosophy to their own lives, the world would be a much better place.

SHAHLA NAEIMI BY STEVE ACEVEDO

Shahla is a gentle, soft, caring woman who has a quiet but dogged determination to carve out a better life for herself and her family in a new land. Her easygoing nature belies her passion to fit in and thrive in her adopted country. Easy to be around, she feels safe and comfortable like those old pair of jeans that you just can't part with.

SHAHLA NAEIMI

I believe that Martin Luther King was one of the most important figures in U.S. history because he stood up for his opinion. He was an "extremist" for what he thought was right.

I will tell you a story of an extreme position I once took. In my country, Iran, approximately 98 percent are Muslim. Because my religion is Bahai, a new faith, the Islamic government persecuted us and disallowed us many rights. The government asked me to deny my faith, for example, if I wanted to study in the university. I really wanted to study, but I'd rather give up education in the university than deny my faith. I remember my classmates' advice, "You can keep your faith in your heart; please just deny it verbally. After finishing your studies, you can go back to your religion." But in my mind, it wasn't acceptable.

I wasn't the only person who would rather keep her faith. A lot of Bahai youth were lynched in the jails or disappeared; their bodies weren't even returned to their families. The government's exclusions made a lot of Iranian Bahais scatter around the world, teaching their faith to others. This exclusion made me emigrate from my home and come to the U.S.A.

MORE STUDENT VOICES

Since the "Transformations" exhibit opened in 2006 and traveled to four other libraries, Venture students have continued to share their voices in public in formal and informal settings. These include Nadia Rivera, mentioned earlier, at a rally for changes in U.S. immigration laws, confronting an angry protestor with a sign, "What Would Jesus Do?," in a photo that appeared on the front page of the *Salt Lake Tribune* in 2011.

Patty Musgrove, a graduate of the Ogden Venture Course, wrote an op-ed for the *Ogden Standard Examiner*, in which she urges others to enroll in the course that changed her life.

> Just when I had decided that there was NOT a way for a person like me to even inch toward a higher education, a miracle landed in my path, designed just for me and many others in our community that are searching for just one little break: a free year-long course consisting of real, transferable, usable college credits—a program designed so that failure is not an option. Its deliberate

set of studies invites a person like myself to engage in the humanities and, in the process, work out our own humanity.[1]

Venture students frequently respond to our request to describe their experiences in the course. We are convinced that they are Venture's best decoders. The following e-mail came from Robin Smith, a Venture graduate. It reflects the perspective of four years after the course, after she graduated from Westminster College and was in the middle of her first year in graduate school:

> As I sit at my desk working on a paper for my graduate course in human development at Loyola University, I pause and "pinch" myself to reflect on how I got here. Venture. I'd always had the "idea" of going to college tucked into a corner of my mind and heart. I saw college as a thing that other people did. Why not me? No resources, no money, no encouragement, and no idea about how "to bridge the gap." Venture was that bridge. The Venture Course in the Humanities gave me the confidence I needed. It said "yes" when everything and everyone else said "no." It said "possible" when the word "impossible" tried to control my mind. The humanities opened up a new world of thinking and relating that finally made sense to me. It taught me new vocabulary and helped me know that I fit into this world just by being. Because of my experience in the Venture Course, I will never again believe in the word "impossible."[2]

ONLINE SURVEYS

Every year—through an anonymous survey online—we ask students to give us feedback about their experience with Venture. They answer specific questions about any changes they see in their choices, their thinking, or their lives, but the most telling responses are those to the open-ended question at the end, which asks them to reflect on what difference Venture has made in their lives:

> Venture has made me feel alive again. I am basically a positive person, but it has been so refreshing and stimulating to be around so

many like-minded people. We—the teachers and the students—all want a better world. By this I mean for each of us individually and as a group to be exposed to new people and ideas, and also discovering a more involved way in relating to this world around us.

I value the Venture program for providing the opportunity for a single parent that hasn't been in a college environment for so long to find courage for myself and my baby girl to take the step to get back into the reading, studying, time management, socializing, communicating, and writing aspect of taking a college course. When I was pregnant, my abusive/criminal husband threatened to take my baby from me. Venture has impacted that threat because now that I am pursuing my educational goals for my own intellect and success, along with instilling education in my daughter, he can never take her from me. Thank you, Venture, for helping me find my inner strength and courage.

I feel more confident in expressing myself in my work, through my writing and in my own words. I have the confidence to return to school, set attainable goals, and believe in myself overall.

I am reminded of my humanity and empathy. Something in life had hardened in me. I feel more like my original self, set again on the right path.

HOPE...I have regained hope in completing all my educational goals from my youth! I'm more positive and feel like I did when I first left home and ventured into this wonderful world. I have many goals, and one has already been achieved: Moving up to a better apartment complex and having my children do better as a result of my attending Venture and seeing me work hard on my schooling. I've been very grateful for having been chosen and given this opportunity, and one of my "secret" goals is to be able to donate monies towards others being able to attend Venture and having this program grow throughout UTAH!!!!

This is the most amazing program. I have a new view on my life and the world around me. I see everything more vividly and with more purpose. Architecture, art, and even the newspaper have become an everyday part of my life. I encourage my son to be more active in his community (school, church, etc.) and that he does have a voice. I am so grateful for this experience. I have said before that in my pursuit of my dream to become a nurse that EVERY nurse should be required to take this program because I feel this will be the foundation of the type of healing professional I want to be. THANK YOU!

In end-of-year and postcourse surveys of alumni, we specifically ask students what in Venture disappointed them. Few reply to the question. We've concluded that the lack of criticism isn't because Venture is a perfect program or met all of their expectations, but because their hunger for education is great. Recent graduates appear to be so grateful for the opportunity Venture provides—and the community they find there—that they dismiss any disappointments they may experience. They leave with hearts and minds full of hope and, years later, remember the change in their lives that began with the Venture Course.

NOTES

1.   Patty Musgrove, "Back to School? Free College! Is That Even Possible?" *Ogden Standard Examiner,* August 18, 2010.
2.   Robin Smith, personal e-mail to Jean Cheney, October 10, 2014.

10

REVERBERATIONS

Venture's Impact

JEAN CHENEY

*The Venture Course changes the future of someone's life. I am among
the people who took the initiative and participated in the course this
year, but the course is really designed for everybody. For those who do
and don't have a job, for those from America, Iraq, Africa, or who are
Native American, or single mothers. From all over the world, we met and
agreed to make the change in our community and our families.*

—AHMED ENAD, *VENTURE GRADUATE*

When we began the Venture Course, we had only a vague idea of its
potential impact. We hoped the course would be meaningful to our students as it had been to those taking the first Clemente Course. When we
were growing up, the five of us who teach in Venture had largely taken
for granted the ways that the humanities became part of us and influ-
enced the directions we took. But we knew that many adults in Utah didn't
have books in their homes as children, or parents who had the leisure,
resources, and education to take them to museums, read newspapers,

and talk about ideas. The economic, social, and educational systems in America create grossly unfair and unequal conditions, leaving many living on low incomes with little chance of having the educational experiences that helped shape our lives.

Even after reading about Earl Shorris's experience in New York, though, we never anticipated the enormous changes this single course would inspire in our students. By April of that first year, students were talking about how Venture had "transformed" them. Some said it was the best thing they had ever done. Not the best course they had ever taken, but *the best thing they had ever done*. What was happening? We had talked about Greek art, Michelangelo, Socrates, Pablo Neruda, the Declaration of Independence, Sandra Cisneros, and Martin Luther King Jr. It wasn't therapy. A lot of times it was hard work. Why were their comments so personal?

The impact hit us, too, in surprising ways. When we gathered at a bar after graduation that first year, our conversation showed our excitement but also our confusion:

"I had no idea that teaching this course would be so satisfying. The students are amazing."

"Even my best classes at the university are not like this. There aren't these breakthroughs or this appreciation. What is going on?"

"When I go to my class in the evening, I'm worn out from the day, not sure what I've got left, and I leave invigorated, inspired. Every single time. The students in class are beautiful."

As with many other questions we've had during the development of Venture, we looked to the students to learn why Venture has such an impact. One came from Anna. In class one night, she said that she loved Venture because it helped her feel free and was a "judge-free zone." She didn't mean that Venture was without rules and restrictions. In fact, course requirements and expectations were clear from the first meeting. "You will not fail," we said, "but only if you stick with it and try." Anna showed up. She wrote. She read. But—she was telling us—through it all, she also felt free.

In her simple statement, Anna condensed volumes of theory describing what a humanities education should be. If you are to search authentically, to test what is true and valid, you must be free to choose, to reject, or to create a new alternative to what you have been taught and not be condemned. You must risk abandoning false ways of being and thinking and be open, have the capacity to challenge ideas and the courage to say what you mean and be who you are. Venture provides a safe place to think and to become.

But there was another component to the Venture experience, one our students described as not gradual, but immediate and intense. At times, it was an epiphany that altered student's sense of themselves and their relationship with their future. Three stories—from Steve, Marcos, and Barbra—helped us understand that studying the humanities provides a light one has been looking for, without realizing it, for a long time.

A handsome, charming forty-year-old man when he came to Venture, Steve—we soon learned—had experienced a rough childhood growing up in the Watts neighborhood of Los Angeles. Discrimination against Hispanics filled the schools he attended and his entire neighborhood but ironically was most intense in his own family. A dark-skinned man, Steve took a backseat to his lighter-skinned older brother. His father seemed to work out his frustrations over discrimination by promoting the ambitions of his eldest son. This light-skinned boy could do no wrong, his youngest son, nothing right. Bigotry operated within the family as cruelly as it did in the outside world.

From the beginning of Venture, Steve was an engaged and engaging student. He charmed us. He wrote well, always had an answer, and made the shyest student laugh. He had it all under control until he met the poet Mary Oliver and "The Journey," the work Jeff uses to introduce poetry in the literature section. As he was reading the poem aloud in class, Steve broke down. He choked on the line, "save the only life you could save." He looked at the class through tears—wordless, for once—and helpless. The class waited in silence.

Months later, talking with his teachers, Steve explained what had hit him so powerfully. While he was growing up, his father had taken his insecurities out not only on his young son but also on his wife, with whom he frequently fought. Sometimes those fights turned violent. After one fight involving a knife when Steve was thirteen, his mother disappeared. He came home from school, and she was gone. His father told him that she had gone away to help a sick relative. As the weeks went by, he began to suspect the truth. His mother wasn't coming back.

Bereft of his greatest ally, Steve faced a host of problems as he grew up. He dropped out of school, although he was an excellent student. He made money and lost it. He went in and out of relationships. When he came to

Venture, he was homeless, couch-surfing with friends, trying to recover from the death of a young daughter.

The poem had reopened the deep childhood wound of his mother's leaving. Was he resentful that we had asked him to read it? "Are you kidding? Reading that poem was one of the most important moments of my life," Steve said. "That poem helped me understand my mother in a way I never had before. She had to leave. She left because she loved us. She did what she had to do. I love that poem." Steve's mother attended his graduation ceremony. She was a small, quiet woman. After the ceremony—when Steve hugged her, holding his certificate—she beamed.

The poem helped Steve release a block that had kept him frozen as a hurt young boy. It is perhaps simplistic to attribute such a life change to the experience of one poem, but Steve does. Some years after he graduated, he wrote a letter to us, recounting his life since finishing Venture, thanking us, and remembering this poem. We posted the letter on the Utah Humanities (UH) website with his permission. It is one person's story of finding happiness and financial security for the first time. It is pure Steve, full of confidence and pride. But there is humility, too. He takes responsibility for his failures. Over the years, Steve has come to Venture graduations, even when he doesn't know anyone graduating. He sits in the back of the auditorium. "I want to congratulate the students," he says. "They've done an amazing thing."

Marcos's epiphany came after writing class one night. As students collected their books and belongings and started to leave the classroom, Marcos approached me, looking uneasy. "What's up?" I asked.

"I don't know how to say this, exactly," he said in a low voice. "It's just that something happened to me in class tonight. I guess it's the critical thinking. What we do in here—in this class and the others—I've never done before, and I really like it. I want more of it, this questioning and figuring out what I really think. I want to be a father someday, and I want to make sure I can do that with my children. How do I make sure that happens?"

Marcos was deadly serious. He liked to joke in class, but he was not joking now. I told him that he could continue to do everything he was doing in class in his private life. He could question and try out answers. He could examine statements for their validity. He could read to learn more before deciding.

But his question caught me off guard, and my answers felt weak. What Marcos had really said was that he was afraid he would lose something that had been born in him. He wanted to nurture it so it wouldn't die. Reassurances were meaningless unless he really did practice on his own what he'd been doing in class.

We hope he will, but we're never sure. We are sure, though, that something important happened to Marcos and changed what he wants for his future. He wants to live as a thinking man. A statement that would have made little sense to him six months ago has now acquired ultimate importance.

Barbra, the student who suffered from lupus and left a religious cult with her three children (she was described in the critical writing chapter) entered Venture with one goal: to set a good example for her children. "I thought my life was finished," she said. "I wanted to do it for them." She had struggled with poverty and lupus for so long that she was exhausted; spent, as she put it, "in all ways a human being can be spent." She would take this course so that her children could see their mother studying. She would show them that if she could do it, so could they.

Then she studied Greek art. She learned about contrapposto in Greek and Roman statues and the exquisite balance of the Parthenon. She studied Greek columns, pediments, and friezes and started seeing them all around her in buildings in Salt Lake City. Suddenly, she could identify the ancient influences on her contemporary world. The thought thrilled her. "I had thought that museums and important buildings were places for rich people, but now I realized that they belonged to me, too," she said. "I could understand them." This was followed by a deeper realization: "Now I wanted this education for me. I wasn't finished. I wasn't washed up. I still had a brain, and I wanted to use it."

Barbra graduated from Venture, then encouraged her daughter, just out of high school, to take the course. After that year, she and her three children enrolled in Salt Lake Community College; all four of them worked on the custodial staff at night to pay for tuition. After earning associate degrees, Barbra and two of her children attended the University of Utah, working on bachelor's degrees.

Steve, Marcos, and Barbra all had sudden realizations in the Venture Course that they were free to choose a different future than the one they had believed was theirs. A different future doesn't necessarily mean a better job or even a college degree. Ends are too often confused with means when it comes to education. These students found the *means* to make changes and grow—what end they work toward isn't as important as the changes that have occurred in the way they think about themselves and the possibilities for their lives.

Through the stories of these three students, we began to realize that Venture students gain immediate—if difficult to measure—benefits from the course, even while they are enrolled. Eventually we came to understand why. When you engage in serious intellectual discussions, you realize that most important questions have more than one answer, often many more. You become comfortable with ambiguity and uncertainty. You learn how to defend your ideas, but because who you are is always respected, you defend them without becoming defensive and are open to changing your mind. You begin to regard yourself as a serious thinker, an identity you may have never tried on before.

It is profound to see your life reflected in great literature, whether it is your tragedies and joys or just the truths of your day-to-day existence. You start to understand that you are not alone. Others have felt and thought what you are feeling and thinking. Or you understand that you *are* alone, and that is the way many people feel. To study the human struggles that run throughout an unvarnished version of American history, visible through primary documents, is to see it as a story of lofty ideals that have often been betrayed. Suddenly, you're able to see the consequences of this history in the lives of people—not in an abstract sense but real people in your community, neighbors, or even people in your family, in yourself.

Because Venture students have their thoughts taken seriously, they begin to think more seriously. Because they are supported by their professors and classmates as they explore ideas and the history of art, they become more skilled as thinkers, speakers, and writers and intellectually more confident. But it's not only a question of skills. The world suddenly becomes more interesting. They identify the influence of the past on the architecture of the buildings they enter, the art that affects them. They understand the philosophical influences on the democracy where they live. They begin to see themselves and their moment in time as part of the great sweep of history. As they feel more connected to the world, the possibilities they imagine for their lives begin to expand.

The impact of all of this doesn't occur sometime in the future for Venture students. It is immediate, and it is powerful. "The Venture Course changes someone's life," wrote Ahmed, a refugee from Iraq. "I am among the people who took the initiative and participated in this course, but the course is really designed for everybody. For those who do and don't have a job, for those from America, Iraq, Africa, or who are Native American, or single mothers. From all over the world, we met and agreed to make the change in our community and our families." After Venture, Ahmed was accepted into Weber State University, where he is studying business.

When Debra was accepted into the Honors College at the University of Utah, she wrote to share her excitement: "I can't thank you enough for the great gift the Venture program was in my life. It's hard not to get emotional when I talk about it. I feel more confident, and I am not afraid to try and get things wrong because I know I won't give up."

Graduates don't always continue in college, but they feel a great change has occurred in them. As Maria wrote, "I wonder if the founders of Venture and teachers really understand the magnitude of what this program means to us. I feel very different after Venture. This has helped me in many different ways like improving my relationships, my capacity to think, write, and learn. It has helped me to adapt to live in this country and to be more optimistic about the future. I think all of this is priceless."

Understanding Venture's power was an affirming experience for the faculty members, but also a humbling and clarifying one. As the course progressed from year to year and we saw the potential of this education, we worried less about course content. Creating a space for exploration and growth became our focus. We still used some of the same readings that had always inspired our students—many of them included in Earl Shorris's first Clemente class—but we worried less about the list than about the ways we encouraged engagement with those texts. Our students taught us that if we did our job—creating a safe space for them to grow as thinkers—they would do theirs, learning from the humanities to better understand themselves and their world. For a student who is ready, studying the humanities can, as one student put it, "rock my world."

While important, the impact of Venture is not limited to personal transformations. Like musical vibrations, we've seen Venture's impact begin with one individual, then extend out to students' spouses and children, to immediate friends and neighbors, to workplaces and communities, and then, through media, to people and groups our students don't even know.

Over the years, many students like Barbra have urged their grown children to take the Venture Course. One year a mother and daughter took the course together. While taking the course, one parent, Alma, let us know that she was urging her younger children to plan on going to college and having them register to take harder courses in high school than they had planned on. As Juanita did when she read "On the Duty of Civil Disobedience," Venture students often tell us that they share readings and class conversations with spouses. When we meet spouses at graduation, who are often carrying bouquets of spring flowers, we see admiration on their faces and a little envy for what their husband or wife has experienced.

One of the best recruitment methods is recommendations from Venture alumni who share their experience with family and friends. "You can take this course, too," they urge. "It's free. It will change your life." Two Venture alumni who worked at a Head Start Center introduced art history into the curriculum after taking Venture. They wanted the three- and four-year-olds in their classes to see the art that had inspired them and learn to speak new names: Rembrandt, Van Gogh, Michelangelo, Frida Kahlo.

Not all of the impact begun by Venture goes smoothly, however. Shaky marriages have split apart after a spouse has taken the course. A couple of years after graduating from Venture, one alumna challenged her employer's discriminatory policies related to her sexual identity. Whether or not she was emboldened by what she had learned about her civil rights in Venture is hard to know, but she voiced her objections and lost her job. She is appealing, but the experience has shown her—and us—that the idealism that Venture encourages needs to be taught along with a heavy dose of realism and awareness of consequences.

In the Venture American history section, Jack Newell requires students to write a letter to a local official or the *Salt Lake Tribune* and to learn their representatives' office phone numbers. We've seen published "Letters to the Editor" from Venture students cover a range of subjects—from education to immigration. One Venture graduate ran for the Salt Lake City Council. He didn't win, but he campaigned with great enthusiasm, dedicated to the issues he believed in. Others have lobbied at the Utah State Capitol in Salt Lake City, preparing their testimonies based on what they've learned in the critical writing, philosophy, and American history sections of Venture.

The Venture Course itself has spread; now two more communities in Utah offer successful Venture courses—Ogden and Cedar City. Each partners with a local university (Weber State University and Southern Utah University, respectively), and local faculty members teach and direct the course. Funding comes primarily from the academic partners with UH continuing to consult on the project and offer minor support. At the time this book was written, more than four hundred students had completed the Venture Course.

In spite of the success we have seen in Venture, we believe it is a weakness in Shorris's Clemente template and ours that the course simply ends at the close of spring semester. Students often feel anxious as graduation approaches, especially those who are uncertain about their next step. Literature professor Jeff Metcalf felt this keenly in 2006 as the first Venture class was ending. As he put it, "To open the door into the wonderful language of the humanities and engage students in such a profound way only to turn them back into the world seemed unfair. Hopefully they had acquired a lifelong set of skills that could help them or enrich their lives, but what if they could continue their experience in some way?"

Sensing that the stories they had shared in class were only the tip of a large iceberg, on an impulse, Jeff asked Venture students one night, "Now that you're almost graduates and know a lot about the power of story and language, would you be interested in learning how to make documentary films and tell your stories in a larger way?" He told them that the class he was imagining would be similar to Venture. It would be taught at night, carry university credit, provide child-care services, assist with transportation costs, and offer a light dinner before class began. Most importantly, it would be free.

Every hand went up.

Fast-forward ten years— Humanities in Focus, a documentary film class, has educated hundreds of students, many of them Venture alumni. Jeff found an Emmy Award–winning filmmaker in Salt Lake City, Craig Wirth, to teach the technical side of the art of filmmaking. Jeff helps students find the story in their lives or their communities they most want to tell. Each year Humanities in Focus brings together students from the community and the Honors College at the University of Utah to make six or seven short documentaries. Since 2007, they have created films about art, drug abuse, a renovated theater, music therapy, domestic violence, homelessness, end-of-life care, gang violence, and scores of other topics. Screenings of the films occur each April in multiple locations throughout the Salt Lake Valley.

Students may reenroll in the course for a second year, and a number of Venture graduates have become so experienced in filmmaking that they now have teaching roles. One, Judy Fuwell, who graduated with a bachelor's degree in communications from the University of Utah, is an expert in film editing and a paid instructor in the program. Another, Lucia Chavarria, teaches the class in Spanish.

Through Judy and Lucia, Venture comes full circle, giving back to the Salt Lake community stories of its people, told by "ordinary citizens" who have learned powerful new ways to use their voices. Once largely invisible in their communities, Venture and Humanities in Focus alumni are now their vibrant interpreters.

The Venture course was also one of a number of factors that moved Utah Humanities (UH) to redefine its mission. Rather than offer one-time humanities programs, UH has decided to focus on partnering with other organizations to "empower individuals and organizations to improve their communities through active engagement in the humanities." Communities may be geographical or cultural, any group that has come together for a reason. Most of UH's programs are not as intensive or sustained as Venture, but Venture helped UH realize that it wanted to be more intentional and focused in its work.

The success of the Venture Course has led to the creation of a high-school version of the curriculum for tenth- and eleventh-grade students who would be the first in their families to attend college. College faculty teach the course with Honors College undergraduate students from the University of Utah and Westminster College. If the pilot program at East High School in Salt Lake City is successful, UH hopes to replicate the course elsewhere in Utah.

The greatest impact the course has had in Utah, though, may be in demonstrating just how important the humanities are to all of us. The humanities should never be regarded as education only for the elite or a luxury only the wealthy can afford. In *The Working Poor,* David Shipler comments that "when the poor or the nearly poor are asked to define poverty. . . they talk not only about what's in the wallet but what's in the mind or the heart."[1]

Venture has shown all of us that one of the best ways to inspire the minds and hearts of people living in poverty is to invite them on a journey with the best writers, thinkers, and artists we can find. These guides will help them determine for themselves what they believe is true and where they want to take their lives. Emboldened by these teachers and the discoveries they make with them, what's in their minds and hearts gets reshaped. In the midst of discouragement, they find courage; from despair, hope.

Will graduates find better-paying jobs? Will they continue with college? Will they engage in politics? Will they be forces for positive change in their communities? Maybe. What most will find, we have learned, is greater agency over their lives. Venture students spend a year having their ideas, writing, and opinions taken seriously. From the moment we shake their hands after their interviews, they join us in a learning community.

Joining a community founded on mutual respect may be the best gift that Venture gives them, and it isn't a gift at all. It is their birthright—what they're entitled to as human beings—but one that their experience may have eroded all confidence in claiming. Once they claim this right, they develop a confidence in their ability to learn, to search for truth, and to grow in ways that no one can take away.

We are not as optimistic as Niecie Walker or Earl Shorris were in believing that rigorous study of the humanities provide a route out of poverty. The social and economic systems that almost assure that poverty continues in the U.S. are deeply entrenched and must be addressed to make real headway. But we are fully convinced that a study of the humanities improves all lives, rich or poor, privileged or oppressed. In Venture, we have found ample evidence that an education in the humanities is an education in hope—for individuals, families, and communities.

But it is more than hope. Open to beauty, emboldened by their power to think critically, alive to the deep truths of story and poetry that connect them to others, students of the humanities can use their understanding to improve their world, one step and voice at a time.

NOTES

1. David K. Shipler, *The Working Poor: Invisible in America* (New York: Alfred A. Knopf, 2004), 7.

EPILOGUE

L. JACKSON NEWELL

A peek into our annual graduation ceremony concludes this tale of Venture's first decade. The ceremony takes place in a bright auditorium on the Westminster College campus, but this venue is the only constant in graduation exercises from year to year. Everything else about our final event varies because it is planned and executed solely by the students. Borrowing a bold notion from Deep Springs College, the faculty made a recommendation toward the end of Venture's first year: "What happens at the graduation ceremony will be up to you. We'll back whatever you choose to do," we told the students. "Just tell us how you wish us to support your ideas."

Students formed a planning committee and chose the speakers, entertainment, and theme—a practice each succeeding class has followed. We encourage them to do most of the speaking, and they typically prevail upon leaders within their ranks to summarize their year and express their gratitude. Among those perennially most appreciated are their classmates, members of their assembled families, and the faculty. The women, especially, thank their children for motivating them to tackle the Venture course: "I felt I had to do this," one said as she gazed out at her three teenage children, "so you will always know how important I believe education is to build a bright future for yourselves."

As students prepared for one of our first graduation ceremonies, Theresa, a shy Latina woman who had blossomed throughout the year, was so daunted when her classmates asked her to speak on their behalf that she agreed only if two others would stand on either side of her at the podium. "I'm petrified," she admitted, "and I need to know that you won't let me crumple if I faint up there."

Two hearty friends stood by Theresa at graduation. She grabbed the rostrum, raised her head, then spoke with an unwavering voice. Her words have blurred with time, but what she expressed remains indelible: pure joy. Joy in encountering noble ideas, in learning to confront scary issues, in finding her own voice, and in looking out to see her two school-age daughters aglow with admiration for the woman their mother was becoming. Our chests were tight with emotion, too.

As Theresa sat down, the spell she had cast over us dissolved as—across the stage—six Japanese *taiko* drummers, friends of one of the students, struck up their deafening beat. The building shook. We all began to sway and clap. Another Venture year was ending with a bang.

Some years later and shortly before he died, Earl Shorris accepted our invitation to fly west and speak at a Venture graduation. After a day of vigorous conversations with faculty and students, he addressed the graduates:

> The reason I am so very grateful to you is that when I first told charitable foundations and universities that I thought this course was a good idea, they usually responded with grace and great wisdom, saying, 'You're nuts.' Well, they may have been right, but not about this. You are not only our students and my friends; we are allies, soldiers together in what we must all consider—more and more—as a war for the soul of America.

He continued,

> Who will save the nation? The burden falls to people who are educated in history and philosophy, on people who have learned to think critically, on people so aware of beauty that it opens their minds to the world, learning to see from the study of art and to sing the most human songs from the study of literature. It is the humanities that give us the great glory of being human, the deepest tragedies teaching us, even as we weep, how to understand the world.

Each Venture year begins on the roof garden of the city library, a band of anxious strangers brought together by little more than a faint hope that something good may come of this course called Venture. Nine months later, it seems those vague dreams have come into focus, hearts are emboldened with new knowledge, and we are joined by a common understanding that our lives—and the decisions we make every day—matter for us and for others. Our voices count, all of them, to shape the kind of world we and our children will inhabit.

ACKNOWLEDGMENTS

There would have been no Venture Course without the help of many people and organizations that stoutly believe that the humanities belong to everyone. We are hugely indebted to Earl Shorris for his brilliant conception of the course in New York City in 1995 and the personal interest he took in Venture, including a trip to Utah in 2011, the year before he died, to speak at Venture graduations in Salt Lake City and Ogden and consult with faculty members. He was a fierce champion of the humanities and all those who embraced the challenge to learn to think for themselves.

We are indebted to Bard College for its wisdom and guidance as we developed Venture, and especially to Marina van Zuylen, academic director for the Clemente Course, for spearheading and hosting annual gatherings of Clemente Course directors at the college each May. We are grateful to Lela Hilton, who is the Clemente Course's national program director and has been a dear friend and wise counselor throughout Venture's life. Lela works hard to strengthen the national network of Clemente courses while respecting the differences within this large, sometimes rambunctious and unwieldy family.

Turning the dream for the Venture Course into reality was made possible by a generous gift from Alternative Visions, a fund of the Chicago Community Trust, and the support of the board and staff of Utah Humanities, especially its executive director, Cynthia Buckingham, and former board chairs Jan Bennett and Irene Fisher. An early gift from Bob Harris allowed us to invite some of the best minds in the Clemente world to travel to Utah in 2006 to consult on our course.

Without the early and steady support of Mary Jane Chase, former dean of arts and sciences at Westminster College, Venture would never have found its first academic home. We are grateful, too, for the personal interest in the course and its students that Westminster College's present dean, Lance Newman, has shown, including securing new scholarships to benefit Venture alumni. We thank James Andersen, former principal of Horizonte Instruction and Training Center, for sharing our vision and providing a home for Venture's first decade. At the University of Utah Honors College, we thank Dean Sylvia Torti, who, together with Dean Newman at Westminster, has supported a high school version of the course at East High School, introducing a new way of studying the humanities to the next generation. Finally, we thank Susan F. Fleming, whose early belief in Venture made all the difference.

We are indebted to Madonne Miner, Forrest Crawford, and Michael Vaughan at Weber State University for shepherding the course along in Ogden, our second partnership; and to Michael Benson, former president of Southern Utah University in Cedar City who, after a conversation with Jean Cheney and Cynthia Buckingham in his office one winter morning in 2010, took about one minute to decide that he wanted his university to be Venture's third home in Utah, a partnership that continues with the steady support of Dean James McDonald and Provost Brad Cook.

Without the concern for Venture students and faculty shown by Shannon Butler, Lindsay Fullerton, Tonia Wilson, Jorge Rojas, Liz Rogers, and Logan Mickel, who all served or currently serve as site directors for the three Venture Courses, the program would never have experienced such robust, healthy development. We are immensely grateful to the past and current Venture faculty in Ogden, Cedar City, and South Salt Lake City for their excellent teaching and genuine concern for their Venture students: Shannon Butler, Elizabeth Dewitte, Michael Hermon, Hikmet Loe, Susan Matt, Marc Nelson, Debi Sheridan, and Tonia Wilson in Ogden; Jodi Corser, Kirk Fitzpatrick, Andy Marvick, Eric Morrow, Earl Mulderink, Ryan Paul, and Jessica Tvordi in Cedar City; and George Henry, Nicholas More, Jeff Nichols, and Nkenna Onwuzuruoha in South Salt Lake City. For her wise consultation with Venture faculty members regarding the best teaching strategies for nontraditional learners, we thank our friend and teacher extraordinaire, Mary Jane Morris.

For his insight in 2006 that students would want to share their work publicly, we thank Kent Miles, whose documentary photography helped us create a traveling exhibit to tell the story of Venture. His generous gift of time and talent enabled Venture students to experience the excitement of "going public" with their work.

We thank the individuals, corporations, and foundations that—in addition to Alternative Visions Fund—have supported Venture over the years, especially the Marriner S. Eccles Foundation, Henry W. and Leslie

M. Eskuche Foundation, Sorenson Legacy Foundation, Richard Jacobsen, George Q. Morris Foundation, CIT Bank, Bridget Newell, and L. Jackson Newell. Their support has allowed the course to thrive.

Finally, we thank John Alley and Glenda Cotter at the University of Utah Press for sharing our belief in the Venture course and supporting our book, an unusual project for the press.

Above all, we are grateful to the more than four hundred students who have taken the risk to join a Venture class for a journey that many continued long after their graduations. Without their joyful curiosity and eagerness to learn, there would be no Venture Course.

BIBLIOGRAPHY

Adler, Mortimer J. *Six Great Ideas.* New York: Touchstone Books, 1997.

Arnold, Matthew. Preface to *Culture and Anarchy: An Essay in Political and Social Criticism,* iii–lx. https://ia801404.us.archive.org/1/items/cultureandanarcooarnogoog/cultureandanarcooarnogoog.pdf.

Cohen, Patricia. "A Rising Call to Promote STEM Education and Cut Liberal Arts Funding." *New York Times,* February 21, 2016. http://www.nytimes.com/2016/02/22/business/a-rising-call-to-promote-stem-education-and-cut-liberal-arts-funding.html?_r=0.

Connell, Jeanne M. "Can Those Who Live in Poverty Find Liberation through the Humanities? Or Is This Just a New Romance with an Old Model?" *Educational Studies* 39, no. 1 (February 2006): 15–26.

Doctorow, E. L. "The Art of Fiction," no. 94. Interview by George Plimpton. *Paris Review* 101 (Winter 1986). http://www.theparisreview.org/interviews/2718/the-art-of-fiction-no-94-e-l-doctorow.

Ellman, Richard, and Robert O'Clair, eds. *The Norton Anthology of Modern Poetry.* New York: W. W. Norton & Company, 1973.

Emerson, Ralph Waldo. "The American Scholar," In *Selected Essays,* 83–106. New York: Penguin Books, 1982.

Erskine, John. *The Moral Obligation to Be Intelligent and Other Essays.* New York: Duffield and Company, 1915.

Freire, Paulo. *Pedagogy of Freedom: Ethics, Democracy, and Civic Courage.* Lanham, MD: Rowman & Littlefield Publishers, 1998.

Gardner, Howard. *Frames of Mind: The Theory of Multiple Intelligences.* New York: Basic Books, 1983.

Hirshfield, Jane. *The Lives of the Heart.* New York: Harper Perennial, 1997.

Housden, Roger. *Ten Poems to Change Your Life.* New York: Harmony Books, 2001.

Johnston, James Scott, and Timothy L. Simpson. "The Use of Socrates: Earl Shorris and the Quest for Political Emancipation through the Humanities." *Educational Studies* 39, no 1 (February 2006): 26–41.

Kessler, Gary E., ed. *Voices of Wisdom: A Multicultural Philosophy Reader.* 6th ed. Belmont, CA: Thomson/Wadsworth, 2006.

MacGregor, Neil. *A History of the World in 100 Objects.* New York: Viking, 2011.

Maslow, Abraham H. *Motivation and Personality.* New York: Harper & Row, 1954.

Merton, Thomas. "Learning to Live." In *Love and Living,* edited by Naomi B. Stone and Brother Patrick Hart, 3–14. San Diego: Harvest/HBJ, 1985.

Musgrove, Patty. "Back to School? Free College! Is That Even Possible?" *Ogden Standard Examiner,* August 18, 2010.

Newell, Bridget M. "Being a White Problem and Feeling It." In *White Self-Criticality beyond Anti-Racism: How Does It Feel to Be a White Problem?,* edited by George Yancy, 121–40. Lanham, MD: Lexington Books, 2015.

Newell, L. Jackson. *The Electric Edge of Academe: The Saga of Lucien L. Nunn and Deep Springs College.* Salt Lake City: University of Utah Press, 2015.

Ng, Jennifer. "Antipoverty Policy Perspectives: A Historical Examination of the Transference of Social Scientific Thought and a Situated Critique of the Clemente Course." *Educational Studies* 39, no. 1 (February 2006): 41–60.

Nussbaum, Martha C. *Poetic Justice: The Literary Imagination and Public Life.* Boston: Beacon Press, 1995.

Nye, Naomi Shihab. *19 Varieties of Gazelle: Poems of the Middle East.* New York: Greenwillow Books, 2002.

Orwell, George. "Why I Write." In *Why I Write,* 1–10. New York: Penguin Books, 2005.

Perry, William G. Jr. *Forms of Intellectual and Ethical Development in the College Years: A Scheme.* New York: Holt, Rinehart and Winston, 1970.

Roberts, Sam. "Jacob Riis Photographs Still Revealing New York's Other Half." *New York Times,* October 22, 2015. http://www.nytimes.com/2015/10/23/arts/design/jacob-riis-photographs-still-revealing-new-yorks-other-half.html?_r=0.

Russell, Bertrand. "On the Value of Philosophy." In *Voices of Wisdom: A Multicultural Philosophy Reader,* edited by Gary E. Kessler, 14–18. 6th ed. Belmont, CA: Thomson/ Wadsworth, 2006.

Shipler, David K. *The Working Poor: Invisible in America.* New York: Alfred A. Knopf, 2004.

Shorris, Earl. *The Art of Freedom: Teaching the Humanities to the Poor.* New York: W. W. Norton & Company, 2013.

———. "On the Uses of a Liberal Education: II. As a Weapon in the Hands of the Restless Poor." *Harper's,* September 1997, 50–59. http://www.harpers.org/archive/1997/09/on-the-uses-of-a-liberal-education/

———. *Riches for the Poor: The Clemente Course in the Humanities.* New York: W. W. Norton & Company, 2000.

Slouka, Mark. "Dehumanized." *Harper's,* September 2009, 32–40. http://www.harpers.org/archive/2009/09/dehumanized.

Strickland, Carol. *The Annotated Mona Lisa: A Crash Course in Art History from Prehistoric to Post-Modern.* 2d ed. Kansas City, MO: Andrews McMeel Publishing, 2007.

Tanka, Judith, ed. *The Norton Anthology of American Literature.* Shorter 6th ed. New York: W. W. Norton & Company, 2003.

Thoreau, Henry David. "On the Duty of Civil Disobedience." In *Civil Disobedience and Other Essays,* 1–20. Reprint, Toronto: Dover Thrift Editions, 1993.

Whitman, Walt. *Democratic Vistas: And Other Papers.* London and Toronto: W. J. Gage & Co., 1888. https://archive.org/stream/democraticvistaoowhitgoog#page/n5/mode/2up

Zinn, Howard. *A People's History of the United States.* New York: Harper & Row, 1980.

THE AUTHORS

Jean Cheney joined the staff of the Utah Humanities Council in 1997 after a career teaching writing and American literature in high schools and universities around the country. In 2005, she founded the Venture Course, now in three Utah locations, and is grateful for the students and faculty who give it life each year. Following one of her passions, she taught environmental writing as a Fulbright scholar at Southwest University in Chongqing, China, in the spring of 2015 and lectured throughout the country on the history of American writing about the land.

L. Jackson Newell served as dean of liberal education at the University of Utah and president of Deep Springs College. He has never missed a year in the classroom or a chance to write. Named the first CASE (Council for Advancement and Support of Education) Professor of the Year in Utah, he also received the national Joseph Katz Award for the Advancement of Liberal Learning. He is currently the Sweet Distinguished Honors Professor for 2016. His most recent work is *The Electric Edge of Academe: The Saga of Lucien L. Nunn and Deep Springs College,* published by the University of Utah Press in 2015.

Hikmet Sidney Loe teaches art history at Westminster College in Salt Lake City. Her research on Robert Smithson's earthwork, *Spiral Jetty,* has led to her book, *The Spiral Jetty Encyclo: Exploring Robert Smithson's Earthwork through Time and Place,* accepted for publication by the University of Utah Press. Friends of Great Salt Lake awarded her its biannual Friend of the Lake Award for her outreach and dedication to issues surrounding Utah's inland sea.

Jeff Metcalf is an award-winning teacher and writer. A professor of English at the University of Utah, he has received the Mayor's Artists Award for Literary Arts, the University of Utah's Distinguished Teaching Award, first place in the Utah Arts Council's Utah Original Writing Competition for his book, *Requiem for the Living: A Memoir,* the University of Utah Outstanding Faculty Award, the John Huntsman Award for Excellence in Education, the National Council of Teachers of English Outstanding Teacher Award, and a Writers @ Work Lifetime Achievement Award.

Bridget M. Newell served previously as associate provost for diversity and global learning and professor of philosophy and gender studies at Westminster College in Salt Lake City. There she established a diversity-focused liberal-education requirement, the Bastian Foundation Diversity Lecture Series, the Diversity & International Center, and the gender studies program. Since 2012, she has been professor of philosophy and associate vice-president for diversity at Bucknell University in Pennsylvania.